*** ALL ***

American

SNACKS

FROM

Hot Dogs

TO

Apple Pie

President: Thomas F. McDow III
Vice-President: Dave Kempf
Managing Editor: Mary Cummings
Project Manager: Tanis Westbrook
Art Director: Steve Newman
Book Design: Jim Scott
Cover Design: David Malone
Typographers: Jessie Anglin, Sara Anglin
Production Coordinator: Powell Ropp

This cookbook is a collection of our favorite recipes, which are not necessarily original recipes.

Published by:
Favorite Recipes® Press
an imprint of

FRP

P.O. Box 305142
Nashville, Tennessee 37230
1-800-358-0560

Manufactured in the United States of America
First Printing 2002   30,000 copies

Contents

Light-Hearted Snacking

In these health-conscious times, we're often confronted with a snack dilemma: how to eat great food that doesn't sabotage our diets. The answer, fortunately, is no longer boring raw veggies with cottage cheese dip. You can indulge in great finger foods without a moment's guilt. We've gathered suggestions for snacks that cut down on fats, sodium or cholesterol without sacrificing flavor and have provided nutritional profiles for all kinds of snacks so you can compare and choose.

Snacks Without GUILT

- Baked potato with low-fat cottage cheese, fat-free cream cheese, mushrooms, green peppers or chopped vegetables instead of butter and sour cream

- Carrot sticks, celery sticks, broccoli or cauliflower instead of chips for dipping

- Salsa or black bean salsa instead of sour cream dip

- Pasta with Parmesan cheese or fat-free dressing

- Pizza with assorted vegetables instead of fat-laden meats and cheeses

- Milk shakes using frozen yogurt and fruit instead of ice cream and toppings

- Popcorn—plain, seasoned with chili powder or Italian seasoning instead of butter

- Dried fruit—apricots, apples, raisins or prunes instead of candy

- Pretzels instead of chips

- Low-fat cottage cheese with chopped tomatoes, green onions and green peppers as a dip

- Onion soup mix with plain yogurt or low-fat sour cream as a dip

- Pita bread with sliced chicken, bean sprouts and fat-free ranch dressing instead of mayonnaise

- Water-pack tuna mixed with pickles, onions and fat-free dressing

- Oven-fried potatoes sliced thin to resemble potato chips

- Baked sweet potato with butter substitute

- Frozen yogurt with fresh fruit, crushed vanilla wafers or crushed gingersnaps instead of nuts

- Boiled new potatoes topped with plain yogurt, low-fat sour cream, green onions or low-fat cottage cheese

- Open-faced toasted cheese sandwiches instead of grilled cheese

- Popsicles—especially those made with fruit juices

- Eggplant dipped in egg wash, rolled in bread crumbs and baked in the oven

- Jelly beans or gummy bears instead of nuts or high-fat candy

- Fig Newtons or vanilla wafers instead of high-fat cookies

- One bite-sized candy bar instead of a large one

Nutritional Profiles of Favorite Snacks

Food Item	Cal	Fat (g)	Prot (g)	Carbo (g)	Sod (mg)
Brie (1 ounce)	95	8	6	<1	178
Cheddar Cheese (1 ounce)	114	9	7	<1	176
Cottage Cheese, low-fat (1 cup)	164	2	28	6	918
Cream Cheese, light (1 ounce)	62	5	3	2	160
Mozzarella Cheese, low-fat (1 ounce)	79	5	8	1	150
Swiss Cheese (1 ounce)	95	7	7	1	388
Ice Cream, vanilla (1 cup)	269	14	5	32	116
Ice Milk, vanilla (1 cup)	184	6	5	29	105
Chocolate Pudding (1/2 cup)	176	5	4	31	514
Vanilla Pudding (1/2 cup)	168	4	4	29	441
Yogurt, frozen (4 1/2 ounces)	118	4	4	19	0
Yogurt, fruit (8 ounces)	225	3	9	42	121
Yogurt, plain (8 ounces)	139	7	8	11	105
Gum Drops (1 ounce)	98	<1	0	25	10
Almond Joy Candy Bar (1-ounce bar)	136	2	2	16	58
Hershey's Candy Bar (1.65-ounce bar)	254	15	4	27	35
Chocolate Chips (1/4 cup)	196	9	2	31	26
Fudge Bar (1 pop)	69	2	2	11	78
Jelly Beans (1 ounce)	104	<1	0	26	3

Nutritional Profiles of Favorite Snacks

Food Item	Cal	Fat (g)	Prot (g)	Carbo (g)	Sod (mg)
Marshmallows (1 large)	19	0	<1	5	2
Corn Chips (1 ounce)	153	9	2	17	218
Potato Chips (1 ounce)	148	10	2	15	133
Graham Crackers (2 squares)	60	2	1	11	66
Ritz Crackers (4 crackers)	70	4	1	9	120
Popcorn, buttered (1 cup)	41	2	1	5	175
Popcorn, plain (1 cup)	23	<1	1	5	0
Pretzels (1 ounce)	111	1	3	22	451
Apple (1 medium)	72	<1	<1	19	0
Apricots, dried (10 halves)	83	<1	1	22	3
Banana (1 medium)	105	1	1	27	1
Grapes (1 cup)	58	<1	1	16	2
Pear (1 medium)	98	1	1	25	1
Raisins ($^2/_3$ cup)	300	1	3	79	12
Chocolate Chip Cookies (2 cookies)	99	4	1	15	84
Oatmeal Cookies (1 cookie)	62	3	1	9	45
Sugar Cookies (2 cookies)	71	3	1	11	51
Fig Newtons (2 cookies)	100	2	1	20	100
Gingersnaps (2 cookies)	59	1	1	11	80
Oreos (3 cookies)	140	6	1	20	170
Vanilla Wafers (5 cookies)	92	3	1	15	50
Jell-O Gelatin ($^1/_2$ cup)	81	0	2	19	54
Apple Pie ($^1/_8$ pie)	282	12	2	43	181
Chocolate Pie ($^1/_8$ pie)	301	17	5	34	311
Angel Food Cake ($^1/_{12}$ cake)	126	<1	3	29	269
Chocolate Cake ($^1/_{12}$ cake)	250	12	3	32	380

Morning Energizers

Breakfast Snack

Yield: 8 to 10 servings

12 eggs
1 pound Cheddar cheese, shredded
1 pound Monterey Jack cheese, shredded
1 (4-ounce) jar salsa

- Beat eggs in bowl.
- Add Cheddar cheese, Monterey Jack cheese and salsa; mix well. Pour into ungreased 9×13-inch baking dish.
- Bake at 350 degrees for 35 minutes.
- Serve warm or cold with muffins and fruit.

Breakfast Tarts

Yield: 30 servings

1 (10-count) can flaky buttermilk biscuits
1/2 cup real bacon bits
16 ounces cream cheese, softened
6 eggs
1/2 teaspoon Season-All salt
1/2 teaspoon pepper

- Separate each biscuit into 3 layers. Place each layer into miniature muffin cups. Sprinkle with bacon bits.
- Combine cream cheese, eggs, salt and pepper in bowl; mix well. Spoon into prepare muffin cups.
- Bake at 350 degrees for 20 to 25 minutes or until set.

Bagel Melt

Yield: 8 servings

4 bagels, halved
8 teaspoons butter
8 slices crisp-fried bacon
1 cup sliced mushrooms
8 slices mozzarella cheese

- Toast bagels.
- Spread each half with 1 teaspoon butter.
- Top with 1 slice of bacon, 2 tablespoons mushrooms and 1 slice mozzarella cheese.
- Broil until cheese melts.

Egg-Asparagus Roll-Ups

Yield: 4 servings

24 fresh asparagus spears
1^1/$_2$ teaspoons lemon juice
5 eggs, beaten
^{1}/$_3$ cup skim milk
1^1/$_2$ tablespoons chopped green onions
^{1}/$_4$ teaspoon salt
^{1}/$_2$ teaspoon pepper
8 (6-inch) flour tortillas
^{3}/$_4$ cup shredded Monterey Jack cheese

- Trim asparagus stems. Steam in vegetable steamer or in microwave until tender-crisp. Toss with lemon juice; set aside.
- Combine eggs, milk, 1^1/$_2$ tablespoons green onions, salt and pepper in bowl; mix well.
- Coat skillet with nonstick cooking spray. Add egg mixture. Scramble until partially set.
- Place damp paper towel between tortillas; wrap in foil.
- Bake at 350 degrees for 5 to 10 minutes or until softened.
- Place 3 asparagus spears in center of each tortilla. Top each with ^{1}/$_8$ of the egg mixture and 1^1/$_2$ tablespoons cheese. Roll up. Place seam side down on serving plates.
- Garnish with warmed salsa, sour cream and additional green onions.

Scrambled Egg and Cheese Sandwiches

Yield: 4 servings

6 eggs
8 ounces cream cheese, softened
1 envelope chicken broth seasoning
1 onion, grated
3/4 cup finely chopped pecans
1 cup cracker crumbs

- Scramble eggs in nonstick skillet. Add cream cheese, stirring until melted.
- Add chicken broth seasoning, onion, pecans and cracker crumbs; mix well.
- Chill in refrigerator overnight or until mixture is firm. Shape into patties. Brown on both sides in nonstick skillet.
- Serve with gravy or tomato sauce. Serve on buns.

Texas Armadillo Eggs

2 cups shredded Monterey Jack cheese
8 ounces hot sausage
1 1/2 cups baking mix
15 jalapeño peppers, seeded
Cheese
1 package Shake 'N Bake for pork
Eggs, beaten

- Combine Monterey Jack cheese and sausage in bowl; mix well with fingers. Add baking mix 1/3 at a time, mixing well after each addition. Mixture will be stiff.
- Stuff peppers with cheese.
- Pat sausage mixture into circles 2 inches in diameter and 1/4 inch thick. Place 1 pepper on each circle. Wrap to enclose pepper completely, pressing edges to seal and shaping to resemble egg. Roll in Shake 'N Bake. Dip in beaten eggs; roll in Shake 'N Bake again.
- Place on baking sheet. Bake at 325 degrees for 20 to 25 minutes or until brown.

English Muffin Breakfast Spread

Yield: 6 servings

1/2 cup maple syrup
1/4 teaspoon nutmeg
1 teaspoon grated orange rind
2 tablespoons milk
3 ounces cream cheese, softened
1/4 cup chopped pecans
6 English muffins, split, toasted

- Combine maple syrup, nutmeg and grated orange rind in small bowl; mix well.
- Combine milk and cream cheese in mixer bowl; beat until soft and creamy. Stir in pecans. Spread cream cheese mixture over toasted side of English muffins; drizzle with syrup mixture.
- May substitute honey for syrup.

Sausage Balls

Yield: 60 servings

1 pound pork sausage
10 ounces baking mix
10 ounces sharp Cheddar cheese, chilled, shredded

- Let sausage stand at room temperature in bowl for 2 hours. Add baking mix; mix well. Mix in cheese. Shape into small balls; place on baking sheet. Bake at 450 degrees for 10 minutes.
- Remove to wire rack to cool.

Smoky Sausage Crescents

Yield: 16 servings

1 (8-count) can crescent rolls
3 ounces cream cheese with chives, softened
2 teaspoons Dijon mustard
1 teaspoon prepared horseradish
1 (5-ounce) package small smoked sausage links

- Unroll crescent roll dough; separate into triangles. Cut each triangle into halves.
- Beat cream cheese in mixer bowl for 2 minutes. Add mustard and horseradish; beat until fluffy. Spread on bottom 2 inches of each triangle. Add sausage link; roll up. Place seam side down on greased baking sheet.
- Bake at 400 degrees for 10 minutes.

Apple Breakfast Dumplings

Yield: 6 servings

2 Granny Smith apples
1 (8-count) can crescent rolls
1/8 teaspoon cinnamon
1/2 cup butter or margarine
1 cup sugar
1 cup orange juice
1 teaspoon grated lemon rind
1 teaspoon vanilla extract

- Peel and core apples; cut into quarters.
- Unroll and separate crescent roll dough. Wrap each piece of apple in 1 crescent roll. Place in 8×8-inch baking dish. Sprinkle with cinnamon.
- Combine butter, sugar and orange juice in saucepan. Bring to a boil. Stir in lemon rind and vanilla. Pour over rolls.
- Bake at 350 degrees for 30 minutes. Spoon pan drippings over rolls when serving.

Applesauce-Cranberry Cupcakes

Yield: 12 servings

1/2 cup melted butter
1/3 cup shortening
1 1/2 cups sugar
4 eggs
2 1/2 cups flour
1 teaspoon cinnamon
1/2 teaspoon baking powder
1 (16-ounce) can cranberry sauce
1 1/2 cups applesauce

- Cream butter, shortening and sugar in mixer bowl until light and fluffy. Add eggs 1 at a time, beating well after each addition. Add flour, cinnamon, baking powder, cranberry sauce and applesauce; mix well. Fill 12 paper-lined muffin cups 2/3 full.
- Bake at 350 degrees for 35 minutes or until cupcakes test done. Remove to wire rack to cool.
- May frost with vanilla frosting.

Cheerio Breakfast Bars

Yield: 24 servings

1/2 cup butter
32 large marshmallows
1/2 cup peanut butter
1/2 cup nonfat dry milk
1/4 cup orange breakfast drink mix
1 cup raisins
4 cups Cheerios

- Melt butter and marshmallows in large saucepan over low heat, stirring to mix well. Stir in peanut butter, milk powder and drink mix. Fold in raisins and cereal.
- Pack mixture into buttered 9×9-inch pan. Let stand until cool. Cut into bars.

Crescent Sweet Rolls

Yield: 15 servings

2 (8-count) cans crescent rolls
1 cup sugar
16 ounces cream cheese, softened
1 egg, beaten
1 teaspoon vanilla extract
3 tablespoons orange juice
Grated rind of 1 orange
1¹/₂ cups confectioners' sugar

- Press 1 can crescent roll dough into 9×13-inch baking dish, sealing perforations.
- Cream sugar, cream cheese, egg and vanilla in mixer bowl until light and fluffy. Spread creamed mixture over roll dough. Top with remaining can crescent roll dough, sealing edges.
- Bake at 350 degrees for 30 minutes. Cut into squares. Drizzle warm rolls with mixture of orange juice, orange rind and confectioners' sugar.

Easy Breakfast Rolls

Yield: 20 servings

2 (10-count) cans biscuits
¹/₂ cup melted butter or margarine
Canned pie filling
2 tablespoons butter or margarine
¹/₄ cup sugar
3 tablespoons flour

- Dip each biscuit into ¹/₂ cup melted butter. Place buttered side up on baking sheet.
- Make indentation in each; fill with favorite pie filling.
- Sprinkle with mixture of 2 tablespoons butter, sugar and flour.
- Bake at 375 degrees for 15 minutes or until golden brown.
- Serve warm.

Noontime Nibbles

Apples and Dip

Yield: 10 to 15 servings

3 teaspoons (heaping) Fruit Fresh
1 tablespoon water
3 yellow Delicious apples
3 red Delicious apples
8 ounces whipped topping
1/2 cup creamy peanut butter

- Mix Fruit Fresh and water in large bowl.
- Cut apples into 1/4-inch slices. Add apples to Fruit Fresh mixture, tossing to coat apples to prevent browning.
- Combine whipped topping and peanut butter in serving bowl; mix well. Place in center of serving plate. Arrange alternating colors of apple slices in circle around bowl of whipped topping mixture on serving plate.
- Serve apples within 6 hours of preparation.
- This dip is also good as ice cream topping.

Cream Cheese Spread for Fruit

Yield: 3 cups

16 ounces cream cheese, softened
1/4 cup butter, softened
1 cup confectioners' sugar, sifted
2 tablespoons orange juice
1 teaspoon grated lemon rind
1 teaspoon vanilla extract
2 pounds apples, sliced

- Combine cream cheese, butter, confectioners' sugar, orange juice, lemon rind and vanilla in bowl; blend well.
- Chill for 30 minutes or longer.
- Place dip in small bowl on serving plate. Arrange apple slices around bowl.

Fireball Cheese Ball

Yield: 1 cheese ball

1 cup shredded Cheddar cheese
3 ounces cream cheese, softened
1 (4-ounce) can deviled ham
2 tablespoons finely chopped onion
3 tablespoons finely chopped green chilies
1/3 cup chopped pecans
Crackers

- Combine Cheddar cheese, cream cheese, deviled ham, onion and chilies in bowl; mix well.
- Shape into ball. Roll in pecans. Wrap in plastic wrap. Chill in refrigerator.
- Serve with crackers.

Peanut Butter Ball

Yield: 1 cheese ball

16 ounces cream cheese, softened
12 ounces creamy peanut butter
3/4 cup confectioners' sugar
1 teaspoon cinnamon
Crushed roasted peanuts
Apple slices
Assorted crackers

- Combine cream cheese, peanut butter, confectioners' sugar and cinnamon in bowl; mix well.
- Shape into ball. Coat with peanuts.
- Chill in refrigerator. Bring to room temperature before serving.
- Serve with sliced apples or crackers.

Praline Cheese Log

Yield: 1 cheese log

8 ounces cream cheese, softened
1/2 teaspoon onion salt or garlic salt
1/4 cup butter
1/3 cup packed light brown sugar
1 teaspoon prepared mustard
2 teaspoons Worcestershire sauce
1/2 cup pecan halves
Assorted crackers

- Combine cream cheese and onion salt in mixer bowl; mix well. Shape into log. Chill, covered, until firm.
- Melt butter in saucepan. Add brown sugar, mustard and Worcestershire sauce. Cook over low heat just to the boiling point. Add pecan halves.
- Spoon half the pecan mixture on foil-lined serving plate. Place cheese log on prepared plate. Spread remaining pecan mixture on top of cheese log. Wrap tightly in foil.
- Chill for 2 to 3 hours.
- Serve on tray with assorted crackers.
- May be frozen and thawed for later use.

Deviled Ham Dip

Yield: 12 servings

2 (4 1/2-ounce) cans deviled ham
2 tablespoons minced onion
1 (6-ounce) jar pimento cheese spread
1 (6-ounce) jar jalapeño cheese spread
1/2 cup mayonnaise-type salad dressing

- Combine deviled ham, onion, cheese spreads and salad dressing in bowl; mix well.
- Chill until serving time.
- Serve with assorted crackers and chips.

Hot Open-Faced Beef Sandwiches

Yield: 10 to 12 servings

3 ounces cream cheese, softened
6 ounces sour cream
1/4 cup finely chopped onion
1/2 cup chopped celery
6 or 7 slices dried beef, chopped
1/2 cup shredded Velveeta cheese
1 large loaf French bread
Butter, softened
Mozzarella cheese, shredded

- Mix cream cheese, sour cream, onion, celery, dried beef and Velveeta cheese in bowl.
- Cut loaf of bread into halves lengthwise. Spread butter over each cut surface. Spread cream cheese mixture over butter; sprinkle with shredded mozzarella cheese.
- Place on baking sheet. Bake at 350 degrees for 10 minutes or until hot and bubbly.

Chinatown Burgers

Yield: 8 servings

1 pound ground beef
1 medium onion, chopped
1 (16-ounce) can bean sprouts, drained
1 (8-ounce) can sliced water chestnuts
1/3 cup soy sauce
1/3 cup water
1 tablespoon molasses
2 tablespoons cornstarch
2 tablespoons water
Salt to taste
Sesame seed buns

- Brown ground beef with onion in skillet, stirring frequently; drain.
- Add bean sprouts, water chestnuts, soy sauce, 1/3 cup water and molasses; mix well. Cook over medium heat for 5 minutes.
- Add mixture of cornstarch and remaining 2 tablespoons water; stir until well blended. Bring to a boil; reduce heat. Simmer for 1 minute. Season with salt.
- Serve on warm toasted sesame seed buns.

Dad's Burgers

Yield: 4 servings

3/4 cup boiling water
1/4 cup bulgur
1/3 cup whole natural almonds
1 pound lean ground beef
1/4 cup chopped green onions
1 teaspoon garlic salt
1 teaspoon basil
4 hamburger buns
4 lettuce leaves
1 tomato, sliced
1 red onion, sliced

- Pour boiling water over bulgur in bowl. Let stand until cool.
- Place almonds in single layer on baking sheet. Bake at 350 degrees for 12 to 15 minutes or until lightly toasted, stirring occasionally. Let stand until cool. Chop coarsely.
- Drain bulgur well. Mix bulgur with almonds, ground beef, green onions, salt and basil in bowl. Shape into patties. Grill over hot coals until cooked through.
- Serve on buns with lettuce, tomato and onion.

Hamburgers on the Grill

Yield: 8 servings

2 pounds ground beef
1 egg, beaten
1/4 teaspoon oregano
1 teaspoon each salt and pepper
1/2 cup catsup
1 tablespoon Worcestershire sauce
1 cup shredded Cheddar cheese
1 cup chopped onion
8 hamburger buns

- Combine ground beef, egg, seasonings, catsup, Worcestershire sauce, cheese and onion in bowl; mix well. Shape into patties.
- Grill over hot coals until cooked through. Serve on buns.

Honolulu Hamburgers

Yield: 4 servings

1 pound ground beef
4 pineapple rings
1/2 cup catsup
1/2 cup packed brown sugar
1/4 cup mustard

- Shape ground beef into 8 patties. Place 1 pineapple ring on half the patties; top with remaining patties, pressing edges to enclose pineapple.
- Combine catsup, brown sugar and mustard in saucepan. Heat to serving temperature, stirring to mix well.
- Grill or broil hamburger patties until cooked through.
- Serve with sauce.

Sloppy Joes

Yield: 6 to 8 servings

1 pound ground beef
1 cup chopped celery
1 small onion, chopped
1 cup tomato sauce
1 cup catsup
2 tablespoons brown sugar
2 teaspoons vinegar
2 tablespoons Worcestershire sauce
2 teaspoons dry mustard
1 teaspoon salt
1 teaspoon pepper
Hamburger buns
1 cup shredded cheese

- Brown ground beef in skillet, stirring until crumbly; drain.
- Stir in celery, onion, tomato sauce, catsup, brown sugar, vinegar and seasonings.
- Simmer mixture for 1 hour or until vegetables are tender, stirring occasionally.
- Serve over hamburger buns; top with cheese.

Beef-Bacon Balls

Yield: 20 servings

1 pound ground beef
1 onion, minced
1/2 green bell pepper, finely chopped
1 1/4 cups bread crumbs
2 eggs, beaten
1 cup canned tomatoes, drained, chopped
1 teaspoon Worcestershire sauce
1 teaspoon prepared mustard
Salt and pepper to taste
8 to 10 slices bacon, cut into halves

- Combine ground beef, onion, green pepper, bread crumbs, eggs, tomatoes, Worcestershire sauce, mustard, salt and pepper in large bowl; mix well. Shape mixture by 1/4 cupfuls into meatballs. Wrap with bacon. Arrange in 9 x 13-inch baking pan so bacon does not touch pan.
- Bake at 350 degrees for 45 minutes; drain. Place on serving dish.

Cheese Fingers

Yield: 30 to 40 servings

1 pound shredded Cheddar cheese
1 1/2 cups butter or margarine, softened
1 1/2 teaspoons dillweed
1 1/2 teaspoons Worcestershire sauce
Dash of cayenne pepper
1 1/2 teaspoons onion powder
1 teaspoon garlic powder
3/4 teaspoon Tabasco sauce
2 loaves sandwich bread, crusts trimmed

- Combine Cheddar cheese, butter, dillweed, Worcestershire sauce, cayenne pepper, onion powder, garlic powder and Tabasco sauce in mixer bowl; mix well. Spread lightly between slices of bread; cut into quarters.
- Spread top and sides of each square with cheese mixture.
- Freeze until firm. Place on baking sheet.
- Bake at 350 degrees for 20 minutes or until golden brown.

Chili Beef Won Tons
Yield: 10 dozen

2 pounds lean ground beef
2 large onions, chopped
4 (4-ounce) cans chopped green chilies
2 cloves of garlic, crushed
1/2 teaspoon oregano
1/2 teaspoon cumin
1 1/2 teaspoons salt
4 cups shredded longhorn cheese
2 (60-count) packages won ton wrappers
Vegetable oil for deep frying

- Brown ground beef in large skillet over low heat, stirring until crumbly; drain.
- Add onions, green chilies, garlic, oregano, cumin and salt; mix well. Cook until onions are golden brown, stirring constantly; remove from heat.
- Add cheese, stirring until cheese melts. Place 1 teaspoon ground beef mixture on each won ton wrapper. Fold as for envelope; moisten edge with water to seal.
- Deep-fry in very hot oil for 12 seconds or until golden brown; drain well.

Fried Cheese Sticks
Yield: 16 servings

1 (8-ounce) package sliced mozzarella cheese
1/4 cup flour
1 egg, beaten
1/4 cup bread crumbs
1/2 cup oil for frying

- Cut cheese slices into halves; roll until cheese forms "sticks." Coat with flour. Dip in egg. Roll in bread crumbs.
- Fry in hot oil in skillet for 1 minute; turn. Fry for 1 minute longer or until golden brown. Drain well.
- Arrange on serving dish.

Toasted Cheese Wraps

Yield: 1 dozen

12 slices white bread
1/4 cup butter, softened
9 ounces Cheddar cheese spread
1/3 cup melted butter

- Trim crusts from bread; discard crusts.
- Combine 1/4 cup butter and cheese spread in bowl; mix well. Spread over bread slices. Roll to enclose filling.
- Place seam side down on baking sheet. Brush with melted butter.
- Bake at 475 degrees for 15 minutes or until golden brown.
- Serve hot. Garnish with watercress and stuffed olives.

Chicken Bundles

Yield: 4 servings

2 cups chopped cooked chicken
8 ounces cream cheese, softened
2 tablespoons butter or margarine, softened
1/4 teaspoon salt
1/8 teaspoon pepper
1 tablespoon onion
2 tablespoons milk
1 (8-count) can crescent rolls
Melted butter
Crushed crackers

- Combine chicken, cream cheese, butter, salt, pepper, onion and milk in bowl; mix well.
- Unroll crescent roll dough. Press 2 triangles together to form a square, sealing perforations.
- Spoon a generous amount of chicken mixture onto square. Bring up sides; seal edges to form ball. Roll in melted butter and crushed crackers.
- Repeat with remaining ingredients. Place on baking sheet.
- Bake at 350 degrees for 20 minutes or until brown.

Curried Chicken Bites

Yield: 42 servings

6 ounces cream cheese, softened
2 tablespoons orange marmalade
2 teaspoons curry powder
3/4 teaspoon salt
1/4 teaspoon white pepper
3 cups chopped cooked chicken
3 tablespoons minced green onions
3 tablespoons minced celery
1 cup finely chopped macadamia nuts

- Combine cream cheese, orange marmalade, curry powder, salt and pepper in bowl; mix well.
- Add chicken, green onions, celery and macadamia nuts; mix well.
- Shape into small balls.
- Chill until serving time.

Chicken in-a-Biscuit

Yield: 4 dozen

3 (5-ounce) cans chicken, drained
1 cup finely chopped celery
1/4 cup finely chopped onion
1/4 cup finely chopped olives
18 hard-cooked eggs, coarsely chopped
3/4 cup (or more) mayonnaise-type salad dressing
48 homemade or canned biscuits

- Combine chicken, celery, onion, olives and chopped eggs in large bowl; mix well.
- Stir in enough salad dressing to moisten.
- Spread filling between biscuits.

Asparagus-Ham Rolls

Yield: 8 servings

8 thin slices ham
4 slices Swiss cheese
1 (15-ounce) can extra-long green asparagus spears, drained
1 (11-ounce) can Cheddar cheese soup
2 tablespoons water
1/4 teaspoon celery salt
Sliced almonds

- Layer each ham slice with 1/2 slice cheese and 2 or 3 asparagus spears.
- Roll as for jelly roll and place seam side down in 8 x 12-inch glass baking dish. Repeat with remaining ham slices, cheese and asparagus spears.
- Spoon mixture of soup, water and celery salt over ham rolls.
- Microwave, covered with plastic wrap, for 5 to 7 minutes. Sprinkle with almonds.

Ham and Cheese Bars

Yield: 36 servings

2 cups baking mix
1/2 teaspoon salt
1/4 cup sour cream
2/3 cup milk
1 egg
1/2 cup chopped onion
2 cloves of garlic, minced
2 tablespoons chopped parsley
3/4 cup chopped smoked ham
1 cup shredded Cheddar cheese
1/2 cup Parmesan cheese

- Combine baking mix, salt, sour cream, milk and egg in mixer bowl; mix well. Add onion, garlic and parsley; mix well. Stir in ham, Cheddar cheese and Parmesan cheese. Spread in greased 9 x 13-inch baking pan.
- Bake at 350 degrees for 25 to 30 minutes or until golden brown.
- Cut into rectangles.

Ham Plus on-a-Bun

Yield: 6 servings

1/2 cup butter or margarine
2 tablespoons chopped onion
2 tablespoons poppy seeds
2 tablespoons prepared mustard
6 hamburger buns, split
6 slices ham
6 slices American cheese

- Combine butter, onion, poppy seeds and mustard in saucepan. Cook over low heat until heated through, stirring frequently.
- Spread mixture on bottom halves of buns. Layer each with 1 slice ham and 1 slice cheese. Replace tops. Wrap each sandwich in foil.
- Bake at 400 degrees for 12 minutes.

Ham and Swiss Cheese Bundles

Yield: 10 servings

1/2 cup butter or margarine, softened
2 tablespoons grated onion
1 tablespoon poppy seeds
1/4 cup Dijon mustard
10 small hamburger buns, split
20 thin slices ham
10 slices Swiss cheese

- Combine butter, onion, poppy seeds and mustard in bowl; mix well. Spread mixture on bottom halves of buns.
- Layer each with 1 slice ham, 1 slice cheese and 1 slice ham. Replace tops. Wrap each sandwich in foil.
- Bake at 350 degrees for 30 minutes.
- May be frozen before baking.

Ham and Spinach-Stuffed Baguette

Yield: 30 servings

1 (24-inch) French bread baguette
8 ounces cream cheese, softened
2 tablespoons lemon juice
2 tablespoons chopped fresh dill
2 green onions, chopped
1 (10-ounce) package frozen chopped spinach, thawed
4 cups minced ham
1/3 cup chopped pecans
1/2 cup mayonnaise
1 tablespoon Dijon mustard

- Cut baguette into halves lengthwise. Scoop out centers, leaving 1/2-inch shells. Wrap loaf tightly with plastic wrap.
- Combine cream cheese, lemon juice, dill and green onions in medium bowl; mix well.
- Squeeze spinach dry. Add to cream cheese mixture; mix well.
- Mix ham, pecans, mayonnaise and mustard in large bowl.
- Coat inside of shell halves and all cut edges with cream cheese mixture. Fill with ham mixture. Place halves together; wrap tightly.
- Refrigerate for 2 to 10 hours before serving. Slice to serve.
- May substitute 1 teaspoon dillweed for fresh dill.

Hawaiian Ham Sandwich

Yield: 6 servings

1 cup ground cooked ham
1/2 cup drained crushed pineapple
1 tablespoon brown sugar
1/8 teaspoon ground cloves
6 raisin-cinnamon bagels, split

- Combine ham, pineapple, brown sugar and cloves in bowl; mix well.
- Spread between bagels.

Mini Ham Sandwiches

Yield: 4 dozen

1/2 cup butter
2 tablespoons onion flakes
1 1/2 teaspoons dried mustard
1 teaspoon Worcestershire sauce
1 1/2 teaspoons poppy seeds
2 (24-count) packages dinner rolls
1 1/2 pounds ham, thinly sliced
1 (18-ounce) package sliced Swiss cheese

- Combine butter, onion flakes, dried mustard, Worcestershire sauce and poppy seeds in small saucepan. Heat until butter is melted; mix well.
- Remove dinner rolls from foil pans; do not separate. Slice dinner rolls into halves. Place ham and cheese on bottom portion. Place top on ham and cheese to form large sandwich. Return to foil roll pans. Pour butter mixture over top of rolls.
- Bake at 350 degrees for 20 minutes.
- Cut rolls into individual sandwiches.

Corn Dogs

Yield: 20 servings

1 pound Monterey Jack cheese
2 (10-count) packages frankfurters
20 soft corn tortillas
1/2 cup oil
3 (16-ounce) cans refried beans

- Cut 20 cheese sticks for frankfurters; shred remaining cheese. Split frankfurters part of the way through. Insert 1 stick cheese into each frankfurter. Wrap each frankfurter with tortilla; secure with wooden pick.
- Fry on all sides in oil in skillet until cheese melts.
- Combine shredded cheese and beans in saucepan. Cook until heated through, stirring constantly.
- Serve as dip for corn dogs.

Frankwiches

Yield: 12 to 16 servings

1 (10-count) package frankfurters, sliced
1 (8-ounce) package shredded mozzarella cheese
2 tablespoons mustard
2 tablespoons pickle relish
1 tablespoon sugar
Catsup
12 to 16 hamburger buns

- Combine uncooked frankfurters slices, cheese, mustard and relish in bowl. Add sugar and enough catsup to coat frankfurters well. Spoon into buns.
- Wrap individually in foil. Freeze if desired.
- Bake at 350 degrees for 30 minutes.

Red Hot Apple Wieners

Yield: 8 servings

4 wieners, chopped
1/2 cup shredded cheese
2 teaspoons chopped onion
1/4 cup catsup
1 cup chopped apple
Butter or margarine
Mustard
8 hot dog buns

- Combine wieners, cheese, onion, catsup and apple in bowl; mix well.
- Spread butter and mustard on hot dog buns.
- Spoon wiener mixture into buns; wrap individually in foil.
- Bake at 350 degrees for 20 minutes.

Pinwheels

Yield: 50 servings

1 cup sour cream
8 ounces cream cheese, softened
1 (4-ounce) can chopped green chilies, drained
1 (4-ounce) can chopped black olives, drained
1/2 cup chopped green onions
1 cup shredded Cheddar cheese
Garlic powder and seasoned salt to taste
5 (10-inch) flour tortillas
Salsa
Parsley

- Combine sour cream, cream cheese, chilies, olives, green onions, cheese, garlic powder and seasoned salt in bowl; mix well. Spread evenly on tortillas. Roll tortillas to enclose filling. Wrap individually in plastic wrap, twisting ends.
- Chill for several hours. Cut each tortilla into 10 slices, discarding ends. Arrange on serving dish with bowl of salsa in center.
- Garnish with parsley.

Mini Pizzas

Yield: 2 dozen

1 pound hot pork sausage
1 pound Velveeta cheese, cubed
2 loaves party rye bread
1 (32-ounce) jar spaghetti sauce

- Brown sausage in skillet, stirring until crumbly. Drain sausage on paper towels.
- Combine sausage and cheese in skillet, stirring until cheese melts. Spread over each slice of party rye bread; top with heaping teaspoonful of spaghetti sauce.
- Bake at 425 degrees for 12 minutes.

Yankee Pizza

Yield: 9 dozen

1 pound bacon, chopped
10 to 12 green onions, minced
1 pound American cheese, coarsely shredded
1 cup mayonnaise
Dash of cayenne pepper
1/2 teaspoon salt
Pepper to taste
2 (12-count) packages dinner rolls with vertical sections

- Cook bacon in skillet over medium heat until edges curl.
- Add green onions. Cook until green onions are tender; drain. Stir in cheese, mayonnaise, cayenne pepper, salt and pepper; mix well.
- Separate rolls vertically into 4 or 5 slices. Roll with rolling pin to flatten. Spread with bacon mixture; place on greased baking sheet.
- Bake at 450 degrees for 5 minutes or until heated through.

Creamy Tuna Garden Wedges

Yield: 16 servings

2 cups baking mix
1/2 cup cold water
8 ounces cream cheese, softened
1/2 cup mayonnaise
1/2 cup sliced green onions
1/8 teaspoon red pepper sauce
2 teaspoons prepared horseradish
1 (6 1/2-ounce) can tuna, drained
2 medium stalks celery
Sliced mushrooms, cherry tomato halves, chopped broccoli and shredded cheese

- Combine baking mix and water in bowl. Beat for 20 strokes. Pat into ungreased pizza pan, forming 1/2-inch rim. Bake at 450 degrees for 10 minutes. Cool.
- Combine cream cheese, mayonnaise, green onions, red pepper sauce, horseradish and tuna in bowl; mix well. Spread over crust. Slice celery diagonally. Outline 6 wedges with celery slices. Top with vegetables and cheese. Chill, covered, for 1 hour. Cut into wedges.

Tuna-Stuffed Eggs

Yield: 6 servings

6 hard-cooked eggs
3 to 4 tablespoons mayonnaise
1 (3¹/₂-ounce) can water-pack tuna, drained
1 teaspoon sweet pickle relish
1 tablespoon prepared mustard
¹/₂ tablespoon grated onion
¹/₈ teaspoon salt
Pepper to taste

- Slice eggs into halves lengthwise. Combine yolks with remaining ingredients in small bowl; mix well.
- Spoon mixture into egg whites.

Super Bowl Sunday Bars

Yield: 60 servings

2 (8-count) cans crescent rolls
2 cups sour cream
1 envelope ranch salad dressing mix
2 cups chopped fresh mushrooms
1 cup chopped tomatoes
1 cup small broccoli flowerets
¹/₂ cup chopped green bell pepper
¹/₂ cup chopped green onions
1 cup shredded sharp Cheddar cheese

- Separate crescent roll dough into 4 long rectangles. Press crosswise over bottom and sides of ungreased 10×15-inch baking pan; press edges to seal.
- Bake at 375 degrees for 14 minutes or until golden brown. Cool completely.
- Combine sour cream and salad dressing mix in small bowl; mix well. Spoon over baked layer.
- Layer with mushrooms, tomatoes, broccoli, green pepper and green onions.
- Sprinkle with cheese. Cut into bars.

Spinach Cheese Puffs

Yield: 50 servings

1 (10-ounce) package frozen chopped spinach
1/2 cup chopped onion
1/2 cup each Parmesan cheese and shredded Cheddar cheese
1/3 cup bleu cheese salad dressing
2 eggs, slightly beaten
2 tablespoons melted butter or margarine
1/8 teaspoon garlic powder
1 (8-ounce) package corn muffin mix
Dijon mustard

- Cook spinach with onion using package directions; drain. Squeeze out excess moisture.
- Combine Parmesan cheese, Cheddar cheese, salad dressing, eggs, butter and garlic powder in bowl; mix well. Stir in spinach mixture and corn muffin mix. Chill, covered, for 1 hour. Shape into 1-inch balls. Arrange on ungreased 10×15-inch baking sheets. Chill until ready to bake.
- Bake at 350 degrees for 10 to 12 minutes or until light brown and heated through. Serve with Dijon mustard. May be frozen and baked for 12 to 15 minutes or until light brown and heated through.

Fresh Strawberry Sandwiches

Yield: 24 servings

1/2 cup butter, softened
1 1/2 cups confectioners' sugar
1/8 teaspoon salt
1/8 teaspoon nutmeg
1 tablespoon vanilla extract
24 slices thin-sliced white bread
1 quart fresh strawberries

- Cream butter in mixer bowl. Add confectioners' sugar gradually, beating well after each addition. Add salt, nutmeg and vanilla; beat until light and fluffy.
- Cut rounds from bread with cookie cutter. Spread rounds with creamed mixture. Chill until serving time.
- Remove stems from strawberries and cut strawberries into thin slices. Arrange overlapping strawberry slices on sandwiches; arrange sandwiches on serving plates. Garnish with fresh mint and whole strawberries.

Afternoon Yummies

Apple Brownies

Yield: 16 servings

2/3 cup butter or margarine, softened
1 cup packed brown sugar
2 eggs
1 teaspoon vanilla extract
1 1/2 cups flour
2 teaspoons baking powder
1/4 teaspoon salt
1 cup chopped apples
1/2 cup chopped nuts

- Cream butter, brown sugar, eggs and vanilla in bowl until light and fluffy.
- Add flour, baking powder and salt; mix well.
- Add apples and nuts.
- Spread into greased 9×9-inch baking pan.
- Bake at 350 degrees for 35 minutes or until edges pull from sides of pan.

Hello Dolly Brownies

Yield: 15 servings

10 tablespoons butter or margarine
1 1/2 cups graham cracker crumbs
1 cup chocolate chips
1 cup coconut
1 (15-ounce) can sweetened condensed milk
1/2 cup chopped pecans

- Melt butter in 9×13-inch baking pan. Press graham cracker crumbs into butter.
- Add layer of chocolate chips and coconut. Pour condensed milk over top; sprinkle with pecans.
- Bake at 350 degrees for 30 minutes. Cut into squares.

Praline Brownies

Yield: 4 dozen

1 (22-ounce) package brownie mix
1/2 cup packed brown sugar
1/2 cup chopped pecans
2 tablespoons melted butter or margarine

- Grease bottom of 9×13-inch baking pan. Prepare brownies using package directions. Spread in prepared pan.
- Combine brown sugar, pecans and butter in bowl; mix well. Sprinkle over batter.
- Bake at 350 degrees for 30 minutes.
- Cool on wire rack. Cut into squares.
- Frost with fudge frosting if desired.

The Ultimate Brownie

Yield: 1 to 11/2 dozen

1 (2-layer) package chocolate cake mix
1 egg, beaten
1/2 cup butter
1 cup chopped pecans or walnuts
1 tablespoon water
8 ounces cream cheese, softened
3 eggs
1 (1-pound) package confectioners' sugar

- Combine cake mix, 1 egg, butter, pecans and water in bowl; mix well. Press into greased 9×13-inch baking pan.
- Combine cream cheese, 3 eggs and confectioners' sugar in mixer bowl; mix until smooth. Pour over chocolate layer.
- Bake at 350 to 375 degrees for 30 to 45 minutes or until golden brown.
- May substitute lemon or yellow cake mix for chocolate if preferred.

Soft Chocolate Chip Cookies

Yield: 4 to 6 dozen

1 cup butter, softened
1 cup oil
1¹/₂ cups packed brown sugar
1¹/₂ cups sugar
4 eggs
2 teaspoons vanilla extract
5 cups flour
2 teaspoons baking soda
1 teaspoon salt
2 cups chocolate chips

- Combine butter, oil, brown sugar and sugar in bowl; mix until creamy. Mix in eggs and vanilla.
- Add mixture of flour, baking soda and salt; mix well. stir in chocolate chips.
- Drop by spoonfuls onto cookie sheet.
- Bake at 350 degrees for 8 to 9 minutes or until golden brown.

Chocolate Kiss Cookies

Yield: 3 dozen

1 cup butter or margarine, softened
¹/₂ cup confectioners' sugar
1 teaspoon vanilla extract
2 cups flour
1 cup finely chopped walnuts
1 (5-ounce) package Hershey's chocolate kisses
¹/₂ cup (about) confectioners' sugar

- Cream butter, ¹/₂ cup confectioners' sugar and vanilla in mixer bowl until light and fluffy. Add flour and walnuts; mix well.
- Shape dough around each chocolate kiss to form a ball. Arrange on ungreased cookie sheet.
- Bake at 325 degrees for 12 minutes.
- Roll warm cookies in ¹/₂ cup confectioners' sugar to coat.
- Cool on wire rack.

Chocolate-Toffee Crescent Bars
Yield: 4 dozen

1 (8-count) can crescent rolls
1 cup packed brown sugar
1 cup butter or margarine
1 1/2 cups chopped pecans
1 cup chocolate chips

- Separate crescent roll dough into rectangles. Press over bottom of 10×15-inch baking pan; press perforations and edges to seal.
- Combine brown sugar and butter in small saucepan. Bring to a boil, stirring constantly. Boil for 1 minute. Pour over dough. Sprinkle with pecans.
- Bake at 375 degrees for 14 to 18 minutes or until golden brown.
- Sprinkle with chocolate chips. Let stand for 2 minutes to allow some of the chocolate chips to melt; swirl melted and unmelted chocolate over top.
- Cool. Cut into bars.

Easy Coconut Macaroons
Yield: 8 dozen

2/3 cup sweetened condensed milk
3 cups shredded coconut
1 teaspoon vanilla extract

- Combine condensed milk, coconut and vanilla in bowl; mix well.
- Drop by teaspoonfuls 1 inch apart onto greased cookie sheet.
- Bake at 350 degrees for 8 to 10 minutes or until light brown.
- Remove macaroons from cookie sheet immediately.

Cornmeal Wafers

Yield: 4 dozen

1/2 cup butter, softened
2/3 cup sugar
1 egg
1 teaspoon vanilla extract
1 cup flour
1 cup yellow cornmeal
1 teaspoon baking powder

- Cream butter and sugar in mixer bowl until light and fluffy. Add egg and vanilla; mix well.
- Mix flour, cornmeal and baking powder together. Add to batter gradually, beating well after each addition.
- Shape into 2 rolls 2 inches in diameter on plastic wrap or waxed paper; wrap securely.
- Chill for 2 hours to 3 days. Cut into 1/8-inch slices with sharp knife. Place 2 inches apart on greased cookie sheet.
- Bake at 325 degrees for 15 to 18 minutes or until golden brown. Remove to wire rack to cool.

I Can't Believe It's A Cookie

Yield: 4 dozen

1 cup sugar
1 cup peanut butter
1 egg
48 chocolate star candies

- Combine sugar, peanut butter and egg in bowl; mix well. Shape into 1-inch balls. Place on cookie sheet.
- Press chocolate star into center of each ball.
- Bake at 350 degrees for 6 minutes.
- Cool on wire rack.

Five-Way Cookies

Yield: 2¹/₂ dozen

1 (14-ounce) can sweetened condensed milk
¹/₂ cup peanut butter
2 cups raisins

- Combine condensed milk, peanut butter and raisins in bowl; mix well.
- Drop by teaspoonfuls onto greased cookie sheet.
- Bake at 375 degrees for 15 minutes or until golden brown.
- Cool on wire rack.
- May substitute 1 of the following for 2 cups raisins: 2 cups cornflakes, 2 cups bran flakes, 3 cups shredded coconut or 1 cup chopped nuts.

Amos' Famous Cookies

Yield: 3 dozen

1 cup margarine, softened
³/₄ cup packed brown sugar
³/₄ cup sugar
1 teaspoon vanilla extract
1 teaspoon water
2 eggs
2¹/₂ cups flour
1 teaspoon baking soda
¹/₂ teaspoon salt
2 cups raisins
2 cups semisweet chocolate chips

- Combine margarine, brown sugar, sugar, vanilla, water and eggs in bowl; beat until creamy. Add flour, baking soda and salt; mix well. Fold in raisins and chocolate chips.
- Drop by teaspoonfuls onto ungreased cookie sheets.
- Bake at 375 degrees for 8 minutes.

Snickers Bar Cookies

Yield: 2 dozen

1 large package refrigerator chocolate chip cookie dough
5 or 6 Snickers candy bars, sliced ¼ inch thick

- Spread cookie dough in 9×11-inch baking pan.
- Bake using package directions or until almost golden brown.
- Arrange candy over baked layer.
- Bake until candy is softened; spread evenly over baked layer.
- Cool. Cut into squares.

Peanut Butter Cups

Yield: 3 dozen

1 (20-ounce) package refrigerator peanut butter cookie dough
1 (14-ounce) package miniature peanut butter cups

- Slice cookie dough; cut slices into quarters. Place each portion in miniature muffin cup.
- Bake using package directions.
- Place 1 miniature peanut butter cup in each cookie.
- Cool in muffin cups.

Chocolate-Peanut Butter Bites

Yield: 12^1/$_2$ dozen

3/4 cup packed brown sugar
1 (1-pound) package confectioners' sugar
2 cups crunchy peanut butter
1/2 cup unsalted butter, softened
2 cups chocolate chips
1 tablespoon unsalted butter

- Combine brown sugar, confectioners' sugar, peanut butter and 1/2 cup butter in bowl; mix well. Pat into ungreased 10×15-inch dish; flatten with rolling pin.
- Melt chocolate chips and remaining 1 tablespoon butter in double boiler over hot water. Spread over peanut butter layer.
- Cut into squares.
- Chill for 15 to 20 minutes; remove from pan.
- Store in refrigerator.

Coconut Balls

Yield: 3 dozen

1 cup creamy peanut butter
1 cup sifted confectioners' sugar
2 tablespoons melted butter or margarine
1/2 cup chopped pecans
1 cup coconut

- Combine peanut butter, confectioners' sugar, butter and pecans in bowl; mix well.
- Shape into 1/2-inch balls. Roll in coconut, coating well.
- Chill in refrigerator.

Coconut Dainties

Yield: 8 dozen

4 cups confectioners' sugar
8 ounces cream cheese, softened
1 cup finely shredded coconut
1 (12-ounce) package colored mints

- Cream confectioners' sugar and cream cheese in mixer bowl until light and fluffy. Stir in coconut.
- Shape into small balls; arrange on waxed paper. Press mint into center of each ball.
- Chill in refrigerator until firm.
- Freezes well.

Fudge-Mallow-Raisin Candy

Yield: 2 dozen

2 cups semisweet chocolate chips
1 cup chunky peanut butter
3 cups miniature marshmallows
3/4 cup raisins

- Melt chocolate and peanut butter in saucepan over low heat, stirring constantly until smooth. Fold in marshmallows and raisins.
- Pour mixture into foil-lined 8×8-inch pan.
- Chill in refrigerator until firm.
- Cut into small squares.

Velveeta Fudge

Yield: 5 dozen

8 ounces Velveeta cheese
1 cup butter
1 1/2 teaspoons vanilla extract
1/2 cup baking cocoa
2 (1-pound) packages confectioners' sugar
1/2 cup nuts

- Combine Velveeta cheese and butter in large saucepan over low heat. Heat until melted, stirring constantly; remove from heat.
- Add vanilla and baking cocoa; blend well. Add confectioners' sugar and nuts; mix well.
- Pour into buttered 9×13-inch pan.
- Chill until serving time.
- Cut into squares.

Peanut Butter Gems

Yield: 9 to 10 dozen

1 cup crunchy peanut butter
3 cups confectioners' sugar, sifted
1 cup melted butter
2 cups semisweet chocolate chips, melted

- Combine peanut butter, confectioners' sugar and butter in bowl; mix well. Pat into 9×13-inch dish. Spread chocolate over top.
- Let stand until firm. Cut into squares.
- Candy freezes well.
- To be sure that others don't polish them off, freeze in empty shortening can with label still intact.

Easy-Do Pralines

Yield: 1¹/₂ dozen

1 (4-ounce) package butterscotch pudding and pie filling mix
¹/₂ cup packed light brown sugar
1 cup sugar
¹/₂ cup evaporated milk
1 tablespoon butter or margarine, softened
1¹/₂ cups pecans

- Combine pudding mix, brown sugar, sugar, evaporated milk and butter in saucepan; mix well. Cook over low heat until sugar is dissolved.
- Add pecans. Simmer until mixture reaches 234 to 240 degrees on candy thermometer, soft-ball stage, stirring constantly.
- Remove from heat. Beat until mixture thickens.
- Drop by spoonfuls onto waxed paper to form 4-inch patties. Let stand until cool.

White Brittle

Yield: 1¹/₂ dozen

1 pound white chocolate
1 cup Spanish peanuts
1 cup broken pretzel sticks

- Melt white chocolate in saucepan. Stir in peanuts and pretzels.
- Spread in thin layer on large tray.
- Chill in freezer until firm.
- Break into pieces.

Evening
Temptations

Beefy Hot Dip

Yield: 50 servings

1 large round loaf bread
1 cup sour cream
8 ounces cream cheese, softened
1 cup shredded sharp Cheddar cheese
3 ounces shredded dried beef
2 tablespoons dried chives
1/2 teaspoon garlic salt

- Cut top from bread; hollow out loaf in shape of bowl, reserving extra bread.
- Combine sour cream, cream cheese, Cheddar cheese, beef, chives and garlic salt in large bowl; mix well. Spoon into bread shell; wrap in foil.
- Bake at 325 degrees for 30 minutes. Break extra bread into small pieces. Add to top of mixture in bread shell.
- Bake for 30 minutes longer.

Spicy Beef Dip

Yield: 60 servings

1 pound ground beef
1/2 cup chopped onion
1 clove of garlic, crushed
1 (8-ounce) can tomato sauce
1/4 cup catsup
1 teaspoon sugar
3/4 teaspoon oregano
8 ounces cream cheese, softened
1/3 cup grated Parmesan cheese

- Brown ground beef with onion and garlic in saucepan, stirring frequently; drain.
- Add tomato sauce, catsup, sugar and oregano. Simmer, covered, for 10 minutes, stirring occasionally.
- Remove from heat. Add cream cheese and Parmesan cheese, stirring until melted.
- Heat to serving temperature over low heat, stirring constantly.

Pacific Northwest Crab Dip

Yield: 15 servings

3 ounces cream cheese, softened
1/2 cup mayonnaise
1 (6-ounce) can crab meat, drained
1/4 cup minced onion
1 tablespoon lemon juice
1/8 teaspoon hot pepper sauce
Small slices French bread or crackers

- Beat cream cheese in mixer bowl until light and fluffy. Add mayonnaise, crab meat, onion, lemon juice and pepper sauce; mix well.
- Spoon into small baking dish.
- Bake at 350 degrees for 30 minutes or until bubbly. Serve with small slices French bread or with crackers.

Herbed Cheese and Shrimp Dip

Yield: 4 cups

3 ounces cream cheese, softened
1/4 cup milk
1/4 cup bottled lemon juice
1/2 teaspoon basil
1/2 teaspoon marjoram
1/2 teaspoon oregano
1/2 teaspoon thyme
1/4 teaspoon garlic powder
1 1/2 cups chopped cooked tiny shrimp
2 whole cooked shrimp
1 green onion top
Assorted crackers and fresh vegetables

- Beat cream cheese in mixer bowl until smooth. Add milk and lemon juice; mix well.
- Add herbs, garlic powder and chopped shrimp; mix well. Spread in 8-inch glass quiche dish.
- Microwave on Medium for 5 to 6 minutes or until heated through. Stir before serving.
- Garnish with whole shrimp and green onion-top fan.
- Serve with crackers or fresh vegetables.

Shrimp Dip

Yield: 40 servings

8 ounces cream cheese, softened
1 (6-ounce) can shrimp, drained
1 bunch green onions, chopped
1 cup Thousand Island dressing
1 (4-ounce) jar chopped pimentos, drained
$1/2$ (7-ounce) jar horseradish
Tabasco sauce to taste

- Combine cream cheese, shrimp, green onions, salad dressing, pimentos, horseradish and Tabasco sauce in serving bowl; mix well.
- Chill until serving time.

Denver Dip

Yield: 12 servings

2 tablespoons mayonnaise-type salad dressing
8 ounces cream cheese, softened
1 tablespoon sugar
8 radishes, finely chopped
2 carrots, finely chopped
1 bunch green onions, finely chopped
1 green bell pepper, finely chopped
Crackers

- Cream mayonnaise, cream cheese and sugar in mixer bowl until light and fluffy.
- Add radishes, carrots, green onions and green pepper; mix well.
- Serve with crackers.

Warm-Me-Up Jalapeño Dip

Yield: 3 cups

8 ounces shredded Colby cheese, at room temperature
8 ounces shredded mozzarella cheese, at room temperature
1/4 cup mayonnaise
2 tablespoons sugar
2 tablespoons finely chopped jalapeño peppers

- Combine cheeses, mayonnaise and sugar in bowl; mix well. Stir in peppers. Add additional mayonnaise to moisten if necessary.
- Serve with crackers.

Nut Roll Dip

Yield: 50 servings

1 (15-ounce) can crushed pineapple, drained
16 ounces cream cheese, softened
1 medium green bell pepper, finely chopped
1 small onion, finely chopped
1 cup finely chopped walnuts
1/2 apple, finely chopped

- Combine pineapple and cream cheese in bowl; mix well. Add green pepper, onion, 1/2 cup walnuts and apple; mix well.
- Shape into a ball. Roll in remaining 1/2 cup walnuts to coat.
- Chill for 2 to 3 hours before serving.
- Serve with butter crackers or potato chips.

Quick Dip
Yield: 20 servings

1 (18-ounce) jar apple jelly
1 (10-ounce) jar pineapple preserves
1 (10-ounce) jar apricot preserves
1 (1-ounce) can dry mustard
1 (5-ounce) jar horseradish
8 ounces cream cheese

- Combine apple jelly, pineapple preserves, apricot preserves, dry mustard and horseradish in bowl; mix well.
- Place cream cheese on serving plate. Pour sauce over top.
- Serve with crackers.

Swamp Dip
Yield: 6 to 8 servings

2 medium tomatoes, finely chopped
1 medium green bell pepper, finely chopped
¹/₂ (4-ounce) can chopped black olives, drained
4 green onions, finely chopped
5 jalapeño pepper slices
Garlic salt to taste
Jalapeño liquid to taste
Tortilla chips

- Combine tomatoes, green pepper, olives, green onions and jalapeño peppers in bowl; mix well.
- Add garlic salt and jalapeño liquid; mix well.
- Serve with tortilla chips.

California Dip Roll-Ups

Yield: 50 servings

1 envelope onion soup mix
2 cups sour cream
2 loaves sliced bread
2 (16-ounce) jars dill pickle spears
Shaved ham and/or shaved smoked turkey
American cheese slices and/or Swiss cheese slices

- Combine onion soup mix and sour cream in bowl; mix well.
- Chill for 2 hours or longer.
- Remove crust from bread; flatten bread with rolling pin.
- Cut pickle spears into halves.
- Spread sour cream mixture on each bread slice. Add ham or turkey, American cheese or Swiss cheese and pickle. Roll to enclose filling.
- Slice each roll into 3 pieces. Pack tightly in covered container.
- Chill until serving time.

Cheesy Spinach Party Loaf

Yield: 2²/₃ cups

1 (1¹/₂-pound) round loaf sourdough bread
¹/₃ cup melted margarine
²/₃ cup chopped red or green bell pepper
¹/₃ cup chopped celery
¹/₃ cup chopped onion
1 pound Velveeta cheese
1 (10-ounce) package frozen chopped spinach, thawed
¹/₄ teaspoon dried rosemary leaves, crushed

- Cut top from loaf; scoop out and reserve center, leaving 1-inch shell. Cut reserved bread into bite-sized pieces. Brush inside of shell with margarine; place loaf on baking sheet.
- Bake at 300 degrees for 20 minutes.
- Sauté pepper, celery and onion in margarine in skillet until tender. Add Velveeta cheese.
- Cook over low heat until cheese melts, stirring constantly.
- Squeeze spinach dry; stir into cheese mixture with rosemary. Pour into bread shell.
- Serve party loaf with reserved bread pieces and assorted fresh vegetable dippers.

Bits o' Broccoli

Yield: 6 dozen

2 (10-ounce) packages frozen chopped broccoli, thawed
2 tablespoons finely chopped onion
3/4 cup shredded low-fat Cheddar cheese
3/4 cup grated Parmesan cheese
2 egg whites, beaten
1 teaspoon garlic powder
1 teaspoon thyme
1/2 cup melted margarine
2 1/2 cups fresh bread crumbs
1/2 cup seasoned Italian bread crumbs

- Drain broccoli well. Combine with chopped onion, Cheddar cheese, Parmesan cheese, beaten egg whites, garlic powder and thyme in bowl; mix well.
- Add margarine and 2 1/2 cups fresh bread crumbs; mix well. Mixture will be very moist.
- Shape into 1-inch balls. Coat with 1/2 cup seasoned bread crumbs. Place 1 inch apart on baking sheet.
- Bake at 350 degrees for 25 minutes.

Cheese Puff Crackers

Yield: 24 servings

1 egg white
1/2 cup shredded Cheddar cheese
1/2 cup mayonnaise
24 round butter crackers

- Beat egg white at high speed in mixer bowl until stiff peaks form. Fold in grated Cheddar cheese and mayonnaise gently.
- Spread mixture on crackers. Arrange on baking sheet.
- Broil until lightly toasted and puffed.

Cheese Nickels

Yield: 6 dozen

1 pound shredded sharp Cheddar cheese, at room temperature
1 cup butter
2 cups flour
2 cups crispy rice cereal
10 dashes of hot pepper sauce

- Combine cheese, butter, flour, cereal and hot pepper sauce in mixer bowl; mix well. Shape into nickel-sized rolls.
- Chill overnight in refrigerator. Cut into thin slices. Place on cookie sheet.
- Bake at 325 degrees for 20 minutes or until golden brown. Remove from oven; sprinkle lightly with salt.

Tasty Cheese Puffs

Yield: 3 dozen

1/2 cup butter or margarine
3 ounces cream cheese, softened
5 to 6 ounces Monterey Jack cheese, shredded
2 egg whites, stiffly beaten
1 large loaf unsliced French bread

- Combine butter, cream cheese and Monterey Jack cheese in top of double boiler over hot water. Cook until melted, stirring frequently. Fold in egg whites.
- Cut bread into cubes. Dip bread into cheese mixture to coat; place on tray. Freeze, covered with waxed paper, until firm.
- Store in plastic bag in freezer. Place cheese puffs on baking sheet.
- Bake at 400 degrees for 8 to 10 minutes or until brown.

Cheese Straws

Yield: 5 dozen

3/4 cup flour
1/2 teaspoon baking powder
1/2 teaspoon dry mustard
Salt and pepper to taste
1/4 cup butter
1/4 cup fine bread crumbs
3 ounces shredded cheese
1 egg yolk

- Sift flour, baking powder, mustard, salt and pepper into bowl. Cut in butter until crumbly. Add bread crumbs, cheese and egg yolk; mix until smooth.
- Roll into 1/8-inch thickness on greased surface. Cut into 1/4×2 1/2-inch straw shapes. Place on greased baking sheet.
- Bake at 400 degrees for 7 to 10 minutes or until golden brown.

Olive-Cheese Snacks

Yield: 30 servings

1/4 cup butter or margarine, softened
1 (5-ounce) jar bacon-cheese spread
3 drops bottled hot pepper sauce
1/4 teaspoon Worcestershire sauce
3/4 cup sifted flour
30 stuffed green olives

- Cream butter and bacon-cheese spread in mixer bowl until light and fluffy. Add hot pepper sauce and Worcestershire sauce; mix well. Add flour; mix to form dough.
- Shape about 1 teaspoon dough around each olive. Place on ungreased baking sheet.
- Bake at 400 degrees for 12 to 15 minutes or until golden brown.

Delicious Chicken Wings

Yield: 30 to 40 servings

30 to 40 chicken wings
1 cup soy sauce
1 (32-ounce) jar apricot jam
6 tablespoons sugar
5 tablespoons lemon juice
2¹/₂ teaspoons ginger
1¹/₄ teaspoons each cinnamon and nutmeg
³/₄ teaspoon allspice
1¹/₈ teaspoons thyme
¹/₈ teaspoon garlic salt

- Disjoint wings, discarding tips. Rinse; pat dry.
- Combine soy sauce, jam, sugar, lemon juice, ginger, cinnamon, nutmeg, allspice, thyme and garlic salt in bowl; mix well.
- Arrange chicken wings in 9×12-inch baking pan. Brush with sauce.
- Bake at 350 degrees for 2 hours or until tender, basting frequently with sauce.
- Serve hot or cold.
- May substitute peach or pineapple jam for apricot jam.

Fruity Dogs

Yield: 6 cups

2 cups apricot preserves
²/₃ cup bottled lemon juice
2 tablespoons cornstarch
1 teaspoon cinnamon
1 (16-ounce) package cocktail franks
1 (16-ounce) can pineapple chunks, drained
2 large red apples, cut into chunks
2 (11-ounce) cans mandarin oranges, drained

- Combine preserves, lemon juice, cornstarch and cinnamon in saucepan; mix well. Cook until thickened, stirring constantly.
- Add cocktail franks and pineapple. Cook until heated through. Add apples and oranges.
- Pour into serving dish. Serve warm.

Hawaiian Grab Bag
Yield: 10 to 12 servings

1 green bell pepper, cut into bite-sized pieces
2 cups cauliflowerets
1 cup small whole fresh mushrooms
1 pint cherry tomatoes
1 cucumber, sliced
2 cups broccoli flowerets
1 avocado, chopped
8 ounces crab sticks, cooked
1 cup shrimp, cooked
3 cups mayonnaise
3/4 cup each sour cream and prepared horseradish
3/4 teaspoon salt
1 tablespoon dry mustard
4 1/2 teaspoons lemon juice

- Combine vegetables, avocado, crab and shrimp in 9×13-inch dish; toss lightly.
- Combine mayonnaise, sour cream, horseradish, salt, mustard and lemon juice in bowl; mix well. Pour over vegetable mixture. Serve with cocktail forks or toothpicks.

Spinach-Stuffed Mushrooms
Yield: 20 servings

1 (12-ounce) package frozen spinach soufflé, thawed
1/3 cup herb-seasoned bread crumbs
1/3 cup grated Parmesan cheese
1/2 teaspoon lemon juice
Dash of hot pepper sauce
20 large fresh mushrooms
2 tablespoons melted butter

- Combine spinach soufflé, bread crumbs, Parmesan cheese, lemon juice and hot pepper sauce in large bowl; mix well. Rinse mushrooms; remove stems. Dip mushroom caps in melted butter. Arrange stem side up in 9×13-inch baking dish.
- Spoon 1 heaping tablespoon of spinach mixture onto each mushroom; drizzle with remaining melted butter. Bake at 400 degrees for 15 to 20 minutes or until filling is puffed.
- Arrange on serving dish; serve hot.

Snow Pea Canoes

Yield: 60 servings

8 ounces Chinese pea pods
3 cups water
Dash of salt
5 ounces cream cheese, softened
6 tablespoons yogurt
1/8 teaspoon pepper
1 teaspoon prepared horseradish
1/2 teaspoon prepared mustard
2 (4-ounce) packages thinly sliced spiced beef, finely chopped

- Trim ends from pea pods. Bring water and salt to a boil in medium saucepan. Add pea pods.
- Simmer over medium heat for 1 minute or until tender-crisp; drain. Immerse in cold water; drain. Chill for 30 minutes or longer.
- Beat cream cheese with yogurt in small bowl. Add pepper, horseradish, mustard and beef; mix well.
- Slit 1 side of pea pods; fill with cream cheese mixture. Place cheese side up in serving dish. Chill for 1 hour before serving.

Onion Crescent Sticks

Yield: 32 servings

2 (3-ounce) cans French-fried onions
2 tablespoons melted butter or margarine
1/2 teaspoon dried parsley flakes
2 eggs, beaten
1/4 teaspoon garlic powder
1 (8-count) can crescent rolls

- Crush French-fried onions in shallow dish. Combine butter, parsley flakes, eggs and garlic powder in shallow dish; mix well.
- Separate rolls into 4 sections; seal perforations. Cut each section into 8 strips. Dip each in egg mixture; coat with crushed onions. Place on greased baking sheet.
- Bake at 375 degrees for 12 minutes or until brown.

Parmesan Cheese Slices

Yield: 10 to 12 servings

1 loaf French bread
1/3 cup butter or margarine, softened
1 bunch green onions with tops, chopped
1 cup mayonnaise
1/2 cup grated Parmesan cheese
1/2 teaspoon Worcestershire sauce
1/2 teaspoon garlic salt
Paprika to taste

- Cut bread into halves lengthwise. Place on baking sheet. Spread cut surfaces with butter.
- Bake at 300 degrees for 10 minutes or until warm.
- Remove from oven; cut into 2-inch slices.
- Spread with mixture of green onions, mayonnaise, Parmesan cheese, Worcestershire sauce and garlic salt. Sprinkle with paprika.
- Broil for 2 to 5 minutes or until brown.

Parmesan Puffs

Yield: 60 servings

1 cup beef broth
1/2 cup butter or margarine
1/2 teaspoon salt
1/4 teaspoon garlic salt
1 cup flour
4 eggs
1/2 cup grated Parmesan cheese
1 tablespoon onion flakes
1 tablespoon Worcestershire sauce

- Combine beef broth, butter, salt and garlic salt in saucepan. Bring to a boil.
- Stir in flour until mixture leaves side of saucepan. Remove from heat; cool slightly.
- Beat in eggs 1 at a time, beating well after each addition.
- Add cheese, onion flakes and Worcestershire sauce; mix well.
- Drop by teaspoonfuls onto greased 10×15-inch baking sheet. Bake at 375 degrees for 20 minutes. Serve warm. May be reheated.

Pepperoni Appetizers

Yield: 15 servings

8 ounces mild Cheddar cheese, shredded
8 ounces mozzarella cheese, shredded
1 (4-ounce) can sliced mushrooms, drained
1 green bell pepper, chopped
1 (4-ounce) can sliced black olives, drained
1 (6-ounce) jar stuffed green olives, sliced
1 cup mayonnaise-type salad dressing
1 (8-ounce) package sliced pepperoni
Tortilla chips

- Mix Cheddar cheese, mozzarella cheese, mushrooms, green pepper, black olives, green olives and salad dressing in bowl. Spread in 9×13-inch dish.
- Top with pepperoni slices.
- Serve with tortilla chips.

New Potato Appetizers

Yield: 24 servings

1/2 cup sour cream
2 tablespoons chopped chives
24 small new potatoes
4 slices bacon, crisp-fried, crumbled

- Mix sour cream and chives together in small bowl; set aside.
- Cook potatoes in boiling water in saucepan until tender; drain. Let stand until cool enough to handle easily.
- Cut into halves; scoop out centers with teaspoon or melon baller. Fill with sour cream mixture; sprinkle with bacon.
- Chill in refrigerator until serving time.
- May add 1/3 teaspoon garlic powder to sour cream mixture.

Crunchy Potato Appetizer Balls

Yield: 8 to 10 servings

2 cups mashed cooked potatoes
2 cups finely chopped ham
1 cup shredded Swiss cheese
1/2 cup mayonnaise-type salad dressing
2 eggs, beaten
1/4 cup finely chopped onion
1 teaspoon prepared mustard
1/2 teaspoon salt
1/4 teaspoon pepper
3 1/2 cups crushed cornflakes

- Combine potatoes, ham, cheese, salad dressing, eggs, onion, mustard, salt and pepper in bowl; mix well. Shape into 1-inch balls. Roll in cornflakes.
- Place on greased 9×13-inch baking sheet.
- Bake at 350 degrees for 30 minutes or until brown.

Faux Champagne Punch

Yield: 18 to 20 servings

1 (2-liter) bottle of sugar-free lemon-lime soda, chilled
1 (12-ounce) can frozen apple juice concentrate
Ice ring
Strawberries or slices of orange, lemon or lime

- Combine soda with thawed apple juice concentrate in large punch bowl; mix well.
- Float ice ring in punch. Garnish with strawberries.

Dry Dock
Yield: 8 servings

1 quart ginger ale, chilled
1 (12-ounce) bottle of Squirt, chilled
1 (12-ounce) can frozen orange juice concentrate, thawed
1/4 cup sifted confectioners' sugar

* Combine ginger ale, Squirt and orange juice concentrate in punch bowl; mix well.
* Add confectioners' sugar; mix well.

Mock Sangria
Yield: 20 servings

1 (12-ounce) can frozen apple juice concentrate
1 (12-ounce) can frozen cranberry juice concentrate
1 (12-ounce) can frozen white grape juice concentrate
1 (12-ounce) can frozen limeade concentrate
2 (2-liter) bottles of diet 7-Up

* Combine apple juice concentrate, cranberry juice concentrate, grape juice concentrate and limeade concentrate in bowl; whisk until smooth. Add 7-Up, stirring until mixed
* Pour into 7-Up bottles to store; fasten caps tightly.
* May be stored indefinitely, tightly capped, in refrigerator.

Pink Lassies

Yield: 6 servings

1 cup cranberry juice
1/4 cup orange juice
1 cup vanilla ice cream

- Process cranberry juice, orange juice and vanilla ice cream in blender until smooth and creamy.
- Pour into glasses.

Tomato Juice Cocktail

Yield: 16 servings

1 gallon tomato juice
2 teaspoons pepper
2 teaspoons salt
1/4 teaspoon Tabasco sauce
2 teaspoons celery salt
1 tablespoon lemon juice
6 tablespoons Worcestershire sauce
1 medium lime
Celery stalk

- Combine tomato juice, pepper, salt, Tabasco sauce, celery salt, lemon juice and Worcestershire sauce in 1-gallon container; mix well.
- Chill in refrigerator.
- Serve with squeeze of lime and stalk of celery.

Happy Endings

Almost Guilt-Free Dessert

Yield: 8 to 10 servings

1 cup seedless grapes
1 cup strawberries
1 cup chopped bananas
1 cup chopped pineapple
1 cup chopped apple
1/2 cup fresh blueberries
2 cups vanilla yogurt
1/2 cup honey
1 teaspoon cinnamon
1/2 cup chopped walnuts or pecans
Coconut to taste

- Combine grapes, strawberries, bananas, pineapple, apple and blueberries in large bowl; toss lightly.
- Combine yogurt, honey, cinnamon, walnuts or pecans and coconut in small bowl; mix well.
- Place fruit in individual bowls. Top with yogurt mixture or dip fruit into yogurt mixture.

Blackberry Fluff

Yield: 10 servings

1 (21-ounce) can blackberry pie filling
8 ounces whipped topping
1 (14-ounce) can sweetened condensed milk
1 (8-ounce) can crushed pineapple
1 cup chopped pecans

- Combine pie filling, whipped topping, condensed milk, pineapple and pecans in large bowl; mix well.
- Chill for several hours to overnight.
- May substitute other flavors of pie filling for blackberry.

Brownie Dessert

Yield: 10 to 12 servings

1 (9×13-inch) pan brownies
¹/₂ gallon coffee ice cream
2 cups fudge sauce
4 Heath bars, chopped
¹/₂ cup chopped pecans

- Cut brownies into squares; place each square on dessert plate. Top each with ice cream, fudge sauce, candy and pecans.
- Serve immediately.

Butterfinger Dessert

Yield: 12 servings

2 eggs
2 cups confectioners' sugar
¹/₂ cup melted butter or margarine
9 ounces whipped topping
2 large Butterfinger candy bars, crushed
1 medium angel food cake

- Beat eggs in mixer bowl. Add confectioners' sugar and butter; beat well. Fold in whipped topping.
- Reserve ¹/₄ of the candy bar crumbs. Add remaining crumbs to whipped topping mixture.
- Tear cake into bite-sized pieces. Alternate layers of cake pieces and whipped topping mixture in 9×13-inch glass dish. Sprinkle with reserved crumbs.
- Freeze until firm.
- To avoid danger of salmonella, use egg substitute instead of fresh eggs.

Butterscotch Crunch

Yield: 16 servings

1 cup flour
¹/₄ cup quick-cooking oats
¹/₄ cup packed brown sugar
¹/₂ cup butter or margarine, softened
¹/₂ cup chopped pecans
1 (12-ounce) jar butterscotch ice cream topping
¹/₂ gallon vanilla ice cream

- Combine flour, oats and brown sugar in bowl. Cut in butter until crumbly. Stir in pecans. Pat into 9×13-inch baking pan.
- Bake at 375 degrees for 15 minutes.
- Stir until crumbly. Cool.
- Remove half the crumb mixture; reserve.
- Drizzle half the topping over remaining crumbs in pan. Spoon ice cream onto top; press down. Sprinkle with reserved crumb mixture. Drizzle with remaining topping. Freeze until firm.
- May substitute chocolate ice cream for vanilla or caramel topping for butterscotch.

Crispy Ice Cream Roll

Yield: 10 servings

¹/₄ cup melted butter or margarine
1 (16-ounce) can vanilla frosting
¹/₄ cup light corn syrup
5 cups crisp rice cereal
1 quart ice cream

- Combine butter, frosting and corn syrup in bowl; mix well. Stir in cereal; coat well.
- Press into waxed paper-lined 10×15-inch pan. Chill for 30 minutes.
- Spread ice cream over cereal mixture.
- Roll as for jelly roll.
- Freeze until firm.

Neapolitan Pound Cake

Yield: 10 servings

1 frozen pound cake, thawed
1 pint Neapolitan ice cream
1 cup hot fudge sauce

- Slice cake into 4 horizontal layers. Cut ice cream into flavors; cut slices into halves.
- Place 1 cake layer on cake plate. Place chocolate ice cream slices on cake layer. Add cake layer and vanilla ice cream slices, another cake layer and strawberry ice cream slices. Top with remaining cake layer.
- Freeze until firm. Cut into slices. Serve with hot fudge sauce.

Caramel Pastries

Yield: 6 servings

1 package Pepperidge Farm frozen pastries
1 cup whipping cream
1 package caramels
3 tablespoons cold coffee

- Bake pastries using package directions. Whip cream in small mixer bowl until soft peaks form. Chill in refrigerator.
- Combine caramels and coffee in top of double boiler. Cook over boiling water until caramels are melted, stirring to mix with coffee. Fill pastries with caramel mixture; top with dollop of whipped cream just before serving.

Pineapple-Orange Parfaits

Yield: 8 servings

1 (6-ounce) can frozen orange juice concentrate, thawed
1/4 cup crushed pineapple
4 cups vanilla ice cream

- Combine orange juice concentrate and crushed pineapple in bowl; mix well.
- Alternate layers of ice cream and pineapple mixture in 8 parfait glasses.
- Store, covered, in freezer. Remove from freezer a few minutes before serving.

American Fruit Pizza

Yield: 12 servings

1 (15-ounce) package refrigerator pie pastry
8 ounces cream cheese, softened
2 tablespoons lemon juice
1/2 cup sugar
1/2 cup whipping cream
Assorted fresh fruit
1/4 cup apricot preserves
1 tablespoon water

- Roll pastry into a 12-inch circle on lightly floured surface. Fit into 10-inch pizza pan. Prick bottom and side with fork.
- Bake at 400 degrees for 9 to 11 minutes or until light brown. Cool.
- Combine cream cheese, lemon juice and sugar in mixer bowl. Beat until blended.
- Add whipping cream. Beat at high speed until light and fluffy. Spread over baked shell. Chill for several hours.
- Arrange assorted fruit over filling. Brush with mixture of preserves and water.

Chocolate Ice Cream Cake

Yield: 16 servings

1 (2-layer) package chocolate cake mix
1 pint chocolate ice cream, softened
3 eggs
1 cup water

- Combine cake mix, ice cream, eggs and water in bowl; mix well. Pour into greased bundt pan.
- Bake at 350 degrees for 45 minutes.
- Cool in pan for several minutes.
- Invert onto serving plate.

Chocolate and Coconut Cake

Yield: 12 servings

1 (2-layer) package devil's food cake mix
3 eggs
1 cup water
1/3 cup oil
2 cups sour cream
1 cup sugar
3 cups coconut
3 cups whipped topping

- Combine cake mix, eggs, water and oil in large mixer bowl; mix well. Pour into 2 greased and waxed paper-lined 9-inch round cake pans.
- Bake at 350 degrees for 35 to 40 minutes or until layers test done.
- Cool. Split each layer into halves.
- Mix sour cream and sugar in bowl. Fold in coconut and whipped topping. Spread between layers and over top and side of cake.
- Chill, covered, in refrigerator for 4 days before serving.

German Chocolate Upside-Down Cake

Yield: 15 servings

1 cup chopped pecans
1 cup coconut
1 (2-layer) package German chocolate cake mix
1/2 cup melted butter or margarine
8 ounces cream cheese, softened
1 (1-pound) package confectioners' sugar

• Mix pecans and coconut in buttered 9×13-inch cake pan, spreading evenly.
• Prepare cake mix using package directions. Spoon into prepared cake pan.
• Combine butter, cream cheese and confectioners' sugar in mixer bowl; mix until smooth. Drop by spoonfuls over batter; spread evenly.
• Bake at 350 degrees for 45 to 50 minutes or until cake tests done.
• Cool on wire rack.

Twinkie Cake

Yield: 12 servings

1 (2-layer) package devil's food cake mix
1/2 cup margarine, softened
1/2 cup shortening
1 cup sugar
3/4 cup evaporated milk
1 teaspoon vanilla extract
1 can Dutch chocolate frosting

• Prepare cake mix using package directions for two 9-inch layers.
• Cool completely. Split layers horizontally.
• Cream margarine and shortening in bowl until light and fluffy. Add sugar; beat until very smooth. Add evaporated milk, beating until fluffy. Beat in vanilla.
• Spread between cake layers.
• Frost with frosting.

Strawberry Surprise Cake

Yield: 8 to 10 servings

1 angel food cake
1 (4-ounce) package French vanilla instant pudding mix
8 ounces cream cheese, softened
1/3 cup milk
1 quart strawberries
16 ounces whipped topping

- Cut off top of cake and reserve. Hollow out bottom, leaving shell. Reserve cake pieces for another purpose.
- Prepare pudding mix using package directions.
- Beat cream cheese with milk in mixer bowl until smooth. Fold into pudding.
- Layer pudding and strawberries 1/2 at a time in cake shell. Replace top.
- Spread whipped topping over top and side of cake.
- Garnish with additional strawberries.

Crazy-Crust Apple Pie

Yield: 6 servings

1 cup self-rising flour
2 tablespoons sugar
1 egg
2/3 cup shortening
3/4 cup water
1 (21-ounce) can apple pie filling
1 tablespoon lemon juice
1/2 teaspoon apple pie spice or cinnamon

- Combine flour, sugar, egg, shortening and water in mixer bowl; beat until smooth. Spread in deep-dish pie plate.
- Mix pie filling with lemon juice and apple pie spice in bowl. Spoon carefully into prepared pie plate; do not mix.
- Bake at 425 degrees until crust is golden brown.

Cheesy Apple Pie

Yield: 6 to 8 servings

1 cup shredded Cheddar cheese
1 recipe 2-crust pie pastry
5 graham crackers, crushed
1/2 cup chopped pecans
2 teaspoons lemon juice
6 cups sliced peeled apples
3/4 cup sugar
2 tablespoons flour
1/2 teaspoon cinnamon
1/8 teaspoon salt
1 cup Cheddar cheese
2 tablespoons butter

- Combine 1 cup cheese and pie pastry in bowl; mix well. Roll on floured surface. Line deep 10-inch pie plate with half the pastry. Sprinkle graham cracker crumbs and pecans in pie shell.
- Sprinkle lemon juice over apples. Combine apples with mixture of sugar, flour, cinnamon and salt in bowl; toss lightly.
- Alternate layers of apples and remaining 1 cup cheese in prepared pie plate, ending with apples. Dot with butter.
- Top with remaining pastry. Seal and crimp edge; cut vents.
- Bake at 450 degrees for 10 minutes. Reduce oven temperature to 350 degrees. Bake for 40 minutes longer. Cool on wire rack.

Caramel Pies

Yield: 12 to 14 servings

1 (24-ounce) package caramels
1/2 cup water
1 cup sour cream
16 ounces whipped topping
2 (9-inch) butter cookie crumb pie shells

- Place caramels and water in saucepan. Cook over low heat until caramels are melted, stirring constantly.
- Let stand until cool. Fold in sour cream and whipped topping. Spoon into pie shells.
- Chill until serving time.

Candy Bar Pie
Yield: 6 servings

1 1/3 cups coconut
2 tablespoons melted butter or margarine
1 teaspoon instant coffee powder
2 tablespoons water
5 (1 1/2-ounce) chocolate candy bars with almonds
4 cups whipped topping

- Combine coconut and melted butter in bowl; mix well. Press over bottom and side of 9-inch pie plate.
- Bake at 325 degrees for 10 minutes or until coconut is golden brown. Let stand until cool.
- Dissolve coffee in water in saucepan over low heat. Melt candy bars in coffee mixture, stirring constantly. Cool slightly. Fold in whipped topping.
- Pour chocolate mixture into prepared pie shell.
- Freeze until firm.

Easy Strawberry Pies
Yield: 12 servings

1 (14-ounce) can sweetened condensed milk
9 ounces whipped topping
Juice of 1 lemon
1/2 cup chopped pecans
1 1/2 cups strawberries
2 graham cracker pie shells

- Combine condensed milk, whipped topping, lemon juice and pecans in bowl; mix well.
- Fold in strawberries.
- Spoon into pie shells.
- Chill until serving time.

Chocoberry-Yogurt Refresher

Yield: 3 servings

8 ounces strawberry yogurt
1 cup chilled milk
1/2 cup sliced fresh strawberries
3 tablespoons Hershey's chocolate syrup
2 tablespoons light corn syrup

- Combine yogurt, milk, strawberries, chocolate syrup and corn syrup in blender container; process until smooth.
- Serve over crushed ice.

Chocolate-Citrus Cooler

Yield: 8 servings

1 1/2 cups chilled milk
1/4 cup thawed frozen orange juice concentrate
3 tablespoons Hershey's Chocolate syrup
1 scoop vanilla ice cream

- Combine milk, orange juice concentrate, chocolate syrup and ice cream in blender container; process until smooth.
- Pour over crushed ice. Top with additional ice cream.

Midnight Munchies

Caramel Apples

Yield: variable

1 (16-ounce) jar caramel ice cream topping
1/2 cup chopped walnuts
Apples
1/4 cup lemon juice

- Warm caramel topping in deep bowl in microwave. Place in center of large platter. Sprinkle walnuts over top.
- Slice apples into wedges; arrange around bowl. Brush apples with lemon juice. Dip apple wedges into caramel.

Midnight Party Mix

Yield: 32 cups

1 cup butter
1 cup margarine
2 tablespoons Worcestershire sauce
4 cups corn bran cereal
4 cups Cheerios
4 cups Spoon Size Shredded Wheat cereal
4 cups Life cereal
1 (8-ounce) bag pretzels
1/2 box (or more) cheese Nip crackers
Salted peanuts
Garlic powder to taste
Powdered Cheddar cheese to taste
Powdered Roma cheese to taste

- Melt butter and margarine in large baking pan. Stir in Worcestershire sauce. Add cereals, pretzels and cheese nips; toss to coat. Add peanuts; mix well.
- Sprinkle with garlic powder and powdered cheeses. Toss to mix.
- Bake at 200 degrees for 21/2 hours.
- Stir every 30 minutes, adding garlic powder and cheeses to desired taste.
- May freeze wrapped in individual packages.

Caramel Corn Chex

Yield: 10 cups

1/2 cup butter or margarine
1 cup packed brown sugar
1/4 cup white corn syrup
Salt to taste
1/2 teaspoon baking soda
10 cups corn Chex cereal

- Combine butter, brown sugar, corn syrup and salt in large saucepan.
- Simmer over medium heat for 5 minutes, stirring constantly. Remove from heat.
- Add baking soda; mix well. Stir in cereal until coated.
- Spread in baking dish. Bake at 200 degrees for 1 hour or until crisp, stirring every 15 minutes. Cool.
- Store in airtight container.

Nibble Mix

Yield: 25 servings

1 cup butter or margarine
1/2 teaspoon garlic salt
1/4 teaspoon minced garlic
1 teaspoon curry powder
1 teaspoon salt
1 teaspoon Worcestershire sauce
Tabasco sauce to taste
5 cups mixed nuts
1 quart popped popcorn
1 (12-ounce) package corn chips
8 ounces small cheese crackers

- Melt butter in roasting pan in oven. Stir in garlic salt, garlic, curry powder, salt, Worcestershire sauce and Tabasco sauce.
- Add mixed nuts, popcorn, corn chips and crackers; toss gently.
- Bake at 250 degrees for 1 hour, stirring occasionally.
- Remove to paper towels to cool.

Niblets

Yield: 12 servings

6 ounces pretzel sticks
1 pound salted peanuts
1 (12-ounce) package rice Chex cereal
1 (12-ounce) package Cheerios cereal
1 tablespoon (scant) garlic salt
1 tablespoon (scant) onion salt
1 tablespoon (scant) celery salt
3 tablespoon Worcestershire sauce
1 cup melted butter

- Combine pretzel sticks, peanuts and cereals in roasting pan. Sprinkle with mixture of garlic salt, onion salt and celery salt.
- Mix Worcestershire sauce with butter. Drizzle over prepared mixture; toss to mix.
- Bake at 225 degrees for 1 hour, stirring every 15 minutes.

Nutty C's

Yield: 25 servings

1 (16-ounce) package wheat Chex
1 (12-ounce) package rice Chex
1 (10-ounce) package Cheerios
1 (12-ounce) package thin pretzels
1 pound mixed nuts
1 pound peanuts
2 cups oil
2 tablespoons Worcestershire sauce
1 teaspoon garlic salt
1 teaspoon seasoned salt

- Mix cereals, pretzels and nuts in large roasting pan.
- Combine oil, Worcestershire sauce, garlic salt and seasoned salt in bowl; mix well. Pour over cereal, mixing gently.
- Bake at 225 degrees for 2 hours, stirring every 30 minutes.
- Cool to room temperature.
- Store in airtight container or plastic bag for up to 2 months.

Banana Confetti Bars

Yield: 35 servings

3/4 cup butter, softened
1 1/4 cups packed brown sugar
1 egg
1 large banana, mashed
1/2 teaspoon lemon juice
1 1/2 cups flour
1/2 teaspoon baking soda
1/4 teaspoon salt
2 cups quick-cooking oats
1 cup "M & M's" Plain Chocolate Candies

- Cream butter and brown sugar in mixer bowl until light and fluffy. Beat in egg, banana and lemon juice. Add mixture of flour, baking soda and salt; mix well. Stir in oats and 1/2 cup candies.
- Spread in greased 10×15-inch baking pan. Sprinkle with remaining candies. Bake at 350 degrees for 25 to 30 minutes or until golden brown. Cool on wire rack. Cut into bars.

Pull Apart S'Mores

Yield: 2 dozen

Peanut butter
24 graham cracker squares
4 cups miniature marshmallows
1 1/3 cups "M & M's" Plain Chocolate Candies

- Spread peanut butter lightly on graham crackers.
- Arrange crackers in single layer in 10×15-inch baking pan. Sprinkle with marshmallows and candies.
- Broil 6 inches from heat source in preheated broiler for 2 minutes or until marshmallows begin to melt.
- Press candies lightly into melted marshmallows. Serve immediately.

Sweet Treats

Yield: 8 cups

3 cups dried banana chips
3 cups thin pretzel sticks
1¹/₂ cups raisins
1¹/₂ cups "M & M's" Peanut Chocolate Candies

• Mix banana chips, pretzel sticks, raisins and candies in bowl. Store in airtight container.

Oyster Cracker Party Mix

Yield: 1¹/₂ pounds

1 (12-ounce) package oyster crackers
1 (8-ounce) package cheese twists
1 package Italian salad dressing mix
1 tablespoon dillweed
2 teaspoons lemon pepper
¹/₄ teaspoon red pepper
2 tablespoons dried parsley
¹/₄ teaspoon garlic powder
¹/₂ teaspoon salt
1 cup oil

• Place crackers and cheese twists onto baking sheet.
• Combine dressing mix, dillweed, lemon pepper, red pepper, parsley, garlic powder, salt and oil in bowl; mix well. Pour over crackers and cheese twists, tossing lightly.
• Bake at 350 degrees for 10 minutes or until light brown, stirring frequently.
• Pour into brown paper bag; shake well.
• Place in serving dish.

Another Oyster Cracker

Yield: 18 servings

1/2 cup sugar
1/2 cup light corn syrup
1/4 cup butter or margarine
1 teaspoon baking soda
1 teaspoon vanilla extract
1 (16-ounce) package oyster crackers
1 cup peanuts

- Cook sugar, corn syrup and butter in saucepan over low heat for 5 minutes. Stir in baking soda and vanilla.
- Place oyster crackers and peanuts in 9×12-inch baking pan. Pour heated mixture over top, stirring to coat crackers and peanuts.
- Bake at 225 degrees for 1 hour, stirring every 15 minutes.
- Break apart to serve.

Peanut Butter Fingers

Yield: 66 servings

1 (1-pound) loaf sliced white sandwich bread
1/2 cup finely chopped peanuts
2 cups creamy peanut butter
1 cup oil

- Allow bread to dry until firm. Trim crusts from bread; reserve for crumbs. Cut bread into 3/4-inch sticks.
- Place breadsticks and trimmed crusts on cookie sheet. Toast at 250 degrees for 1 1/4 hours or until crisp and brown.
- Cool. Crumble crusts and 2 breadsticks into fine crumbs. Combine crumbs with peanuts in shallow dish; mix well.
- Blend peanut butter and oil in bowl. Dip breadsticks into peanut butter mixture; roll in crumb mixture to coat.
- Place on waxed paper. Let stand until dry.

Rocky Road Pizza

Yield: 12 servings

1 cup butter, softened
1/2 cup sugar
1/2 cup packed brown sugar
1 egg
1 teaspoon vanilla extract
1 3/4 cups flour
1 cup peanuts
1 cup marshmallows
1 cup semisweet chocolate chips

- Cream butter, sugar and brown sugar in mixer bowl until light and fluffy. Beat in egg and vanilla. Add flour gradually, beating constantly at low speed.
- Spread evenly in ungreased 14-inch pizza pan.
- Bake at 375 degrees for 12 minutes. Sprinkle peanuts, marshmallows and chocolate chips on top.
- Bake for 6 to 8 minutes longer or until marshmallows are golden brown.

Caramel Corn Crunch

Yield: 10 servings

1/2 cup butter
1 cup packed brown sugar
1/2 teaspoon baking soda
1 teaspoon vanilla extract
2 cups buttered popped popcorn
1/2 cup mixed nuts
1/2 cup Crispix
1/2 cup Cheerios

- Combine butter and brown sugar in saucepan. Simmer over low heat for 5 minutes, stirring constantly. Remove from heat.
- Stir in baking soda and vanilla.
- Combine popcorn, nuts and cereals in large bowl; mix well. Add butter mixture; toss to coat. Spread in large baking dish.
- Bake at 300 degrees for 1 hour, stirring every 15 minutes.

Harvest Popcorn
Yield: 11 cups

6 tablespoons melted butter
1 teaspoon dillweed
1 teaspoon lemon pepper
1/2 teaspoon garlic salt
1/2 teaspoon onion powder
1 teaspoon Worcestershire sauce
2 quarts popped popcorn
2 cups shoestring potatoes
1 cup mixed nuts

- Combine butter, dillweed, lemon pepper, garlic salt, onion powder and Worcestershire sauce in bowl; mix well.
- Place popcorn, shoestring potatoes and mixed nuts in large bowl; mix well.
- Pour butter mixture over popcorn mixture; toss to coat. Spread into baking pan.
- Bake at 350 degrees for 6 minutes, stirring once.

Honey Oven Popcorn
Yield: 20 cups

1 cup honey
1 cup packed brown sugar
1 cup butter or margarine
1 teaspoon salt
1/2 teaspoon baking soda
1 cup peanuts
5 quarts popped popcorn

- Combine honey, brown sugar, butter and salt in saucepan. Simmer over low heat for 2 minutes, stirring constantly. Remove from heat. Add baking soda.
- Combine with peanuts and popcorn in large baking dish.
- Bake at 250 degrees for 1 hour, stirring occasionally.

Peanut Butter Popcorn

Yield: 14 cups

3 quarts popped popcorn
1¹/₂ cups nuts
1 cup sugar
¹/₂ cup honey
¹/₂ cup light corn syrup
1 cup peanut butter
1 teaspoon vanilla extract

- Mix popcorn and nuts in baking dish. Keep warm in 250-degree oven.
- Combine sugar, honey and corn syrup in saucepan. Simmer over medium heat for 2 minutes. Remove from heat.
- Add peanut butter and vanilla, stirring until well blended. Pour over popcorn mixture.
- Spread on baking sheet. Cool.

Puppy Chow

Yield: 3 pounds

2 cups chocolate chips
¹/₂ cup butter
1 cup creamy peanut butter
1 (12-ounce) box Crispix
1 (1-pound) package confectioners' sugar

- Melt chocolate chips and butter in saucepan.
- Blend in peanut butter. Add cereal; toss to coat.
- Coat with confectioners' sugar.

Potato Stick Snack

Yield: 14 servings

1 (3-ounce) can French-fried onions
2 cups rice Chex cereal
1 (4-ounce) can potato sticks
3/4 cup Spanish peanuts
1/4 cup melted butter
1/2 envelope taco seasoning mix

- Combine onions, cereal, potato sticks and peanuts in 9×13-inch baking pan.
- Drizzle with butter; toss gently to mix. Sprinkle with taco seasoning mix; mix well.
- Bake at 300 degrees for 30 minutes, stirring occasionally.
- Cool. Store in airtight container.

Dipped Pretzels

Yield: 1 pound

1 (12-ounce) package almond bark
1 (9-ounce) package small pretzels

- Melt almond bark using package directions.
- Dip pretzels into melted almond bark. Place on waxed paper.
- Let stand until firm.

Onion Pretzels

Yield: 10 servings

1 (18-ounce) package pretzels
1 cup butter or margarine
1 envelope onion soup mix

- Break pretzels into bite-sized pieces.
- Melt butter in 4-quart saucepan. Add soup mix; mix well.
- Add pretzels gradually, stirring to coat well. Spread on 10×15-inch baking sheet.
- Bake at 225 degrees for 45 minutes, stirring every 15 minutes.

Scramble

Yield: 50 servings

1 pound cashews
1 pound mixed nuts
1 pound pecan halves
1 (12-ounce) package wheat Chex
1 (12-ounce) package round oat cereal
2 (8-ounce) packages pretzel sticks
2 cups oil
1 teaspoon garlic salt
1 tablespoon seasoned salt

- Combine cashews, mixed nuts, pecans, cereals, pretzels, oil, garlic salt and seasoned salt in large roasting pan; mix gently with wooden spoon.
- Bake at 250 degrees for 2 hours, stirring every 15 minutes.
- Cool to room temperature. Store in airtight container.
- May substitute sesame sticks for round oat cereal and rice Chex for wheat Chex if preferred.

Snax
Yield: 50 servings

4 cups rice, corn or wheat Chex
16 ounces oyster crackers
2 cups Doo-Dad crackers
2 cups pretzels
2 cups cheese Duck crackers
1 1/2 cups salad oil
2 envelopes buttermilk salad dressing mix
1 teaspoon lemon pepper
1 teaspoon dillweed
1 teaspoon garlic powder

- Combine cereal, oyster crackers, Doo-Dads, pretzels and cheese Ducks in bowl.
- Blend oil and salad dressing mix in small bowl. Add seasonings; mix well. Pour over cereal mixture; mix well. Spread on baking sheets.
- Bake at 250 degrees for 15 to 20 minutes or until warm.

Southwestern Munch
Yield: 16 cups

2 (3-ounce) cans French-fried onions
4 cups corn Chex
2 cups Cheerios
1 1/2 cups Spanish peanuts
2 (4-ounce) cans shoestring potatoes
2 cups rice noodles
2 1/2 ounces slivered almonds
1/2 to 3/4 package dry taco seasoning mix
1/2 cup melted butter or margarine

- Combine French-fried onions, cereals, peanuts, shoestring potatoes, rice noodles, almonds and taco seasoning in large bowl; mix well.
- Add butter; toss to coat mixture. Spread in large baking pan.
- Bake at 250 degrees for 30 minutes, stirring every 10 minutes to avoid burning French-fried onions.

Fake Strawberries

Yield: 2 to 3 dozen

1 (6-ounce) package strawberry gelatin
1 (3½-ounce) can coconut
2 cups finely chopped pecans
1 (14-ounce) can sweetened condensed milk
Red sugar
Green sugar

- Combine gelatin, coconut, pecans and condensed milk in bowl; mix well.
- Chill until firm. Shape into strawberries.
- Roll in red sugar; dip 1 end in green sugar.

Sweet Crispix Mix

Yield: 12 servings

2 (12-ounce) packages Crispix cereal
2 cups pecan halves
2 cups almonds
1 cup butter
2 cups packed light brown sugar
1 cup dark corn syrup
1½ to 2 teaspoons vanilla extract

- Combine cereal, pecan halves and almonds in roasting pan sprayed with nonstick cooking spray.
- Melt butter in medium saucepan. Add brown sugar, stirring until dissolved. Stir in corn syrup. Bring to a boil over low heat, stirring constantly; remove from heat. Stir in vanilla. Pour over cereal mixture; toss to coat.
- Bake at 250 degrees for 1 hour, stirring every 15 minutes.
- Spread on 10×15-inch baking sheets. Cool. Break into large pieces.
- Store in airtight container.

Television Mix

Yield: 20 servings

1 (12-ounce) box wheat Chex
1 (12-ounce) box Cheerios
1 (12-ounce) box rice Chex
1 (8-ounce) package small thin pretzels
2 teaspoons seasoned salt
2 (8-ounce) cans mixed nuts
1 (8-ounce) can peanuts
1 (8-ounce) can pecans
1 tablespoon garlic salt
2 cups oil

- Combine cereals, pretzels and seasoned salt in bowl; mix well.
- Stir in mixed nuts, peanuts, pecans and garlic salt. Pour in oil; toss to coat mixture. Spread into large baking dish.
- Bake at 250 degrees for 2 hours, stirring several times.
- Cool. Store in airtight container.

Triple Goodness

Yield: 8 servings

6 ounces butterscotch chips
1¹/₂ cups golden raisins
1¹/₂ cups salted peanuts

- Combine butterscotch chips, raisins and peanuts in bowl; mix well.
- Spoon into 8 small plastic bags

My Favorite Trash

Yield: 12 servings

$^1/_2$ cup butter
13 ounces nutella (hazelnut spread)
2 teaspoons almond extract
1 (14-ounce) package honey-graham Chex cereal
1 pound dark raisins
8 ounces chopped dates
4 cups mixed nuts
2 cups semisweet chocolate chips
1 (1-pound) package confectioners' sugar

- Melt butter in small saucepan. Add nutella and almond extract; mix well.
- Combine cereal, raisins, dates, mixed nuts and chocolate chips in heavy-duty plastic bag. Pour nutella mixture over top; shake to coat. Add confectioners' sugar; shake to coat. Store in airtight containers to prevent moisture.
- May substitute peanut butter for nutella. do not use chemically treated plastic bags.

White Chocolate Delights

Yield: variable

Butter crackers
Peanut butter
White chocolate

- Spread half the crackers with peanut butter; top with remaining crackers.
- Melt chocolate in double boiler over hot water. Dip cracker sandwiches into chocolate to coat. Place on waxed paper or wire rack to dry.

White Chocolate Candy

Yield: 25 servings

2 pounds white chocolate
1 cup peanut butter
3 cups crisp rice cereal
1 (24-ounce) jar dry-roasted peanuts
1 (10-ounce) package marshmallows

- Melt white chocolate and peanut butter in saucepan, stirring to mix well. Combine with cereal, peanuts and marshmallows in large bowl; mix well.
- Drop by spoonfuls onto waxed paper. Let stand until firm.
- Store in airtight container.

Yum-Yum

Yield: 20 servings

3 cups Special-K cereal
1 cup packed brown sugar
1/2 cup coconut
1/2 cup melted butter
1/2 gallon ice cream
1 (16-ounce) can chocolate syrup

- Combine cereal, brown sugar, coconut and butter in bowl; mix well.
- Press into 9×13-inch dish.
- Soften or slice ice cream; spread over cereal mixture. Top with chocolate syrup.
- Freeze until firm.

Index

Published by:
Favorite Recipes® Press
an imprint of

FRP™

P.O. Box 305142
Nashville, Tennessee 37230
1-800-358-0560